I Believe in Angels

THE MIRACULOUS TRUE STORY OF
CATASTROPHIC VEHICLE COLLISION
SURVIVOR ASHLEY

W. L. Adams

TRILOGY CHRISTIAN PUBLISHERS

TUSTIN, CA

Trilogy Christian Publishers
A Wholly Owned Subsidary of Trinity Broadcasting Network
2442 Michelle Drive
Tustin, CA 92780

For information, address Trilogy Christian Publishing

Rights Department, 2442 Michelle Drive, Tustin, Ca 92780.

Trilogy Christian Publishing/ TBN and colophon are trademarks of Trinity Broadcasting Network.

For information about special discounts for bulk purchases, please contact Trilogy Christian Publishing.

Manufactured in the United States of America

Trilogy Disclaimer: The views and content expressed in this book are those of the author and may not necessarily reflect the views and doctrine of Trilogy Christian Publishing or the Trinity Broadcasting Network.

10 9 8 7 6 5 4 3 2 1

Library of Congress Cataloging-in-Publication Data is available.

ISBN 978-1-64773-314-8

ISBN 978-1-64773-315-5 (ebook)

Contents

This book is dedicated to my beautiful daughter Ashley.

Never forget you are loved.

Your life has significant purpose.

Special Thanks

Jesus, my wonderful Lord and Savior. My three children: Ashley, Ariel, and Jacob. You are loved immensely. Thank you for being very patient with me and for loving me unconditionally.

Thank you to every road crew, rescue worker, and health care provider, as well as every soul who prayed for my family and graciously touched our lives in a positive manner during the onset of this case.

Through laughter and tears, being able to recite a true-life testimony of the amazing, miraculous healing power of God is certainly worth it. I am eternally grateful. Humble thanks. God bless each and every one of you.

Introduction

God is omnipresent: He is always present everywhere, continuously and simultaneously present throughout the entirety of creation within this galaxy and other realms. God is everywhere, present all the time, and can be found anywhere. God is the sole supreme being, the Creator and the Author of *all* creation.

God is omnipotent: He is all-powerful, possessing complete, unlimited, universal power and authority. God is love. God is a sovereign being.

What are angels? Angels are powerful spiritual beings, a separate creation of God's, made before mankind. They are mentioned in holy Scripture more than a hundred times. Angels are not of this world; they are heavenly beings from another realm, having the God-given ability to enter in as well as exit from one realm into another, although the holy Scriptures suggest that the kingdom of heaven is as close as our very breath. The heavenly beings, including archangels, ministering angels, seraphim, and cherubim, were created long before mankind. No human knows how many angels actually exist. Their purpose varies on the type of angel they are. There are angels that guard the throne of God, angels that are warriors, angels that are ministering angels, angels that are messengers, angels that report to God, giving an account of how an individual is doing, and angels that simply carry forth an assignment that is delegated to them by God. Their encounters with human beings have been accurately archived all the way back to biblical times within the holy Scriptures. Since those days, over the course of more than two thousand years, orthodox churches as well as other authors have archived mind-staggering testimonies of humans claiming to have experienced an encounter with God Himself or a heavenly messenger of some sort, while also noting that such experiences happen to be very uncommon.

Perhaps you, too, have experienced an encounter with one of these heavenly beings. If you have, or if you know someone who has, we're a part of a very small group of individuals within this century, whom God has personally chosen to grace with the extraordinary. Such encounters are rare. God has a special purpose for your life. God has entrusted you, or perhaps someone you know, among a world filled with countless doubters, scoffers, and nonbelievers of this generation, with an awesome testimony. That in and of itself is a blessing. Never feel discouraged to talk about it. Your testimony just might be the type of encouragement another person needs during the struggle they're going through.

"Do not neglect to show hospitality to strangers, for by this some have entertained angels without knowing it..."

—Hebrews 13:2 NASB

Prologue

Ashley was born two months early, on Christmas morning, in the year 1985. On the morning of her birth, I almost hemorrhaged to death. Moments before her birth, I asked the medical team to address Ashley's medical needs before my own. We both were at risk of losing our lives. Once she was born and brought into this world as a fragile premature infant, she was immediately placed in an incubator within the hospital nursery. While the healthcare team addressed her immediate medical needs, I lay silent in a recovery room and then went unconscious, ultimately requiring a blood transfusion. During the time I was unconscious, I communed with God. In His presence, I felt surrounded in perfect love as well as peace. I would have loved to stay there, had God not advised me that it was not yet my time. And like the child I was at the time, at the tender age of sixteen, standing at the threshold of heaven, I pleaded with God to allow me to stay there with Him. He assured that I wouldn't require medical treatment after He returned me to this realm. I didn't want to return to this world. Yet God returned me back to this world anyway, confirming that my assignment here was not yet over, validating that it truly is God who has the last word with regard to life as well as death.

The moment I awakened, a medical provider was positioned at my left, advising me that I had "lost a lot of blood and required a blood transfusion." Although, I almost bled to death that morning, I refused to receive a blood transfusion, while recollecting my conversation with God. At first, the medical provider appeared concerned. Yet his countenance changed to that of awe as he listened intently as I described what it was like to commune with Jesus. The healthcare team honored my rejection of the blood transfusion that day, while my older sister, Lisa, stood at the right side of my hospital bed, weeping. Nonetheless, I miraculously survived, completely trusting in what my heavenly Father had advised, while in fellowship with Him. That evening, on Christmas 1985, I was not yet strong enough to walk. Therefore, the nurses pushed my hospital bed into the nursery, next to Ashley's incubator, where I held her tiny little right hand for a few moments. I wept tears of joy. The medical team had been successful at saving both of our lives. Ashley was so tiny and frail, connected to many medical wires and tubes. I noticed my maternal grandmother and step-grandfather standing in the hospital corridor, staring through the nursery window, while observing both of us. I was returned to my assigned hospital room down the hallway a few moments later, and then I was released from the hospital the following day. My newborn premature infant was hospitalized for several weeks beyond the date of her birth, receiving routine gavage (tube) feedings by mouth. She was unable to be breastfed or bottle-fed because her mouth was so small. Although Ashley was born premature, with a low birth weight, she eventually was released from the hospital nursery to finally go home once she could receive bottle feedings and had reached the adequate weight of five pounds. She quickly caught up to those who were the same age as her.

Despite the fact that Ashley had been born out of wedlock, she was a very vibrant, athletic, and talented young lady. She was raised up in the Christian faith, she believed in angels, and she was very much a "Mommy's girl." She enjoyed sports and had a natural artistic talent. She had plenty of friends of varied ethnicities as well as backgrounds, and she enjoyed family gatherings. She was a novice musician, having learned to play three instruments; the clarinet, the viola, as well as acoustic guitar.

I'm so thankful God returned me to this world, enabling me to have a part in raising Ashley, as well as to give birth to my two other children.

Ashley is the eldest of five siblings; a sister and a brother, she has from me. Their names are Ariel and Jacob. The other two siblings, brothers Kellen and Caden, are from her biological dad and his significant other out in the Midwest. She was an incredible help to her younger siblings while they were still small.

Ashley, W.L. Adams, & Ariel in the summer, 1994.

Amongst a church congregation in southern California, Ashley was selected for a part within a Christian video that was never released: *Junior Soldiers for Jesus Christ*, through the church we attended. Both Ashley and her younger sister, Ariel, starred in that faith-based video.

Ashley was actively involved in sports as well as extracurricular activities, including softball, cheerleading, soccer, and FCCLA, to name a few. She enjoyed swimming as well as beach excursions and participating in aquatic sports. She attended school in both the states of Idaho and California. She graduated high school, right on time, in the year 2004, and she started college a few months later, with the intent to eventually become an entrepreneur and owner of her own day spa.

Jacob & Ashley, at Lake Elsinore, CA, in the summer of 2004.

Only a few days before Ashley was in her vehicle collision, she disclosed that she had had a "vision" of a bright light and then a cloud hovering over her, while she was lying in bed resting in our residence. Unalarmed, I sat down and prayed with my daughter. I opened up the pages of holy Scripture to her, advising her that perhaps her "vision" was the Shekinah glory, and I showed her the reference within my Bible. Ashley was amazed, deciding in that moment that was what she wanted to name her future day spa. Unfortunately, she wasn't capable of finishing college and attaining that goal as an entrepreneur. However, she's very thankful to still be alive.

Ashley proudly wears a "True Love Waits" ring, based on a decision she made before her vehicle collision in 2004. On occasion, she donates her hair to an organization that makes wigs for cancer patients, an organization she had learned of shortly after the turn of the millennium.

Ashley is a daughter, a granddaughter, a sister, a niece, a cousin, a friend, an inspiration, a miracle, and a child of God. She enjoys good food, good music, polite conversation, as well as family gatherings.

Ashley as a high school student, 2004.

"A day in the presence of God is as a thousand years. And a thousand years as one day."

—2 Peter 3:8

Two Worlds Collide

On Sunday morning, October 10, 2004, while I was getting myself and my two youngest children prepared to attend church, my eldest child, Ashley, took me aside to inform me she wouldn't be able to attend church that day, as she was scheduled to work. Ashley had recently graduated from high school and had started attending beauty college, with the intent to open her own day beauty spa someday. She also worked at a part-time job at a clothing store in our local mall. I advised her that I understood if she wouldn't be able to attend church that day and told her she could catch a midweek evening service, scheduled at the church we attended. Or, I said, perhaps she could attend one of the Bible studies that I had recently started hosting in our home, along with a few other church members, a part of the same congregation.

Ashley nodded in agreement and then asked if I'd consult with her youth pastor, Pastor Ken, on her behalf. She had decided to recite the salvation prayer and become a follower of Jesus Christ. She wanted her youth pastor and I to arrange her water baptism. Smiling, I said to my teenaged daughter, "Absolutely. Amen. Praise God!" Ashley smiled back at me. We hugged one another, and then she left for work.

The following day, Monday, October 11, 2004, while her siblings were at school, Ashley accompanied me to a local Christian charity that operated in the same town we resided in. She assisted with unloading a van filled with lightly used baby items as well as children's clothes. While we were there, we noted that the Republicans had a gathering across from where we were standing, and so we decided to visit their committee. We enjoyed brief conversation with a few of the individuals. A very energetic Ashley voiced the political issues that she was in favor of as well as opposed to, with unmistakable enthusiasm. The Republican ladies listened with great adoration, welcoming both Ashley and me to join their future meetings. Then Ashley decided to register to vote, excitedly advising everyone present of her intention to vote for George W. Bush during the upcoming presidential election. She proceeded to grab a stack of his campaign stickers. This would be the first time my daughter had had the opportunity to vote within her lifetime.

On the way home, my very ecstatic daughter started peeling the paper from the back of each campaign sticker, while affixing them to the inside of the cabin of my vehicle. I asked her to stop, reminding her that the campaign stickers were supposed to be placed on the outside of the vehicle to promote Bush's campaign. She giggled with great zeal. Ashley's enthusiasm didn't surprise me, since she was a former cheerleader. I also knew that she had been blessed with the charismatic gift of *helps* from the time she was very young. I was glad to learn of the political issues she was in favor of as well as opposed to. I believed she had a good head on her shoulders and was already making wise decisions as a young adult.

Moments later, we pulled into a fast-food restaurant drive-thru. Ashley chatted away about a Halloween prank she had in store for her aunt, who lived in the same neighborhood. Ashley disclosed her intentions of purchasing a life-size character cardboard cutout from a local movie rental place. She advised the character was her aunt's favorite from the film. Ashley said, "I'm going to purchase that cardboard cutout, place a Ho-Ho hat [a Santa Claus hat] on it, and position it directly in front of Aunt Lisa's front door. Then I'm going to ring the doorbell, run, and hide. Do you think she'll get mad?" I said, "Probably. She won't even tolerate us toilet-papering her house and yard." Then we both laughed for a moment. Ashley claimed that she planned to follow through with her prank regardless. I responded, "Okay, let me know how she reacts."

On the morning of Tuesday, October 12, 2004, Ashley had decided to stay home from college. She had gotten up early and allowed me to sleep in, while tending to the care of her three-year-old brother, Jacob. She had fed him breakfast and had gotten him dressed by the time I rolled out of bed. My other daughter, Ariel, was thirteen years old at the time, and she had already left to attend her regularly scheduled classes out at the local junior high school. My husband at the time had already left for work. As I quietly walked down the stairs, I could see both Ashley and Jacob nestled on the sofa, watching a children's program together in the family room. Once Ashley discovered that I was awake and making my way down the staircase, she jumped up immediately and started walking graciously in my direction, almost appearing to be gliding. She was smiling, and I noted that she, too, was already dressed for the day, in a denim miniskirt, a pastel-green V-line T-shirt, layered over her favorite white strap T-shirt, with a butterfly adorned in the center, an ensemble that I had purchased for her as a gift the previous Christmas.

She escorted me to the kitchen, proudly announcing she had packed three suitcases. We were planning to relocate that afternoon with my other two children (Ashley's siblings), since things weren't going well at home with my spouse. I was experiencing marital difficulties and had requested a legal separation from my husband the previous evening. I thanked Ashley for helping. Then she advised me that she had made her "first pot of coffee" that morning, while bringing my attention to the kitchen countertop where she had daintily set two merlot rose–decorated coffee cups on their coordinating saucers, along with a coordinating sugar bowl and cream service set. She had also neatly positioned two silver teaspoons next to each place setting for both of us. That's when we both noticed that the brewed coffee along with the coffee grinds were spilling over and out of the carafe onto the countertop. Ashley quickly started to clean up the spill, while apologizing. I smiled and explained that the carafe simply needed to be positioned correctly within the coffeemaker compartment to prevent this from occurring. She and I then proceeded to enjoy a single cup of coffee together, conversing, while sitting outdoors in the front patio area.

While Ashley and I sat outside, she advised me that she was planning to meet her boyfriend out for breakfast that day. I asked her to wait until I could get ready to leave. I offered to treat her and her boyfriend out for breakfast that morning. Ashley sort of rolled her eyes at me, politely refusing my offer, advising me that she and her boyfriend wanted to have breakfast alone with one another, without the distraction of her mother and three-year-old brother. I silently stared at her for a few moments, studying her facial expression before finally insisting they have me present. I didn't much care for the boy Ashley was dating at the time, and he was well aware of that. What I didn't like about that guy was that he never spoke to me, when he visited my home to pick my daughter up for a date. I'd attempt to start a conversation with him. He wouldn't respond. I thought his act of ignoring me, in my residence, while I tried to start a conversation with him, in a cordial manner, was pretty darn rude. The other thing I didn't like was that he borrowed my daughter's accessories. I thought out loud, "There's something wrong with that guy!" Then I asked my daughter, "Do you have plans of marrying him?" Ashley simply laughed.

At about that moment, our conversation was interrupted as she noticed the neighbor's handsome son (who was a firefighter) pushing his new motorcycle out from his parent's garage. Immediately, Ashley jumped up from where she was sitting, ecstatic that the neighbor's son had purchased a motorcycle. Looking in the direction of the boy next door and at the change in my daughter's countenance, I said, "Uh-huh... Why not ask the boy next door for a ride before he leaves?" However, Ashley was too shy to speak with him. And then we both watched him disappear on his motorcycle. After he was out of view, Ashley sat back down and disclosed to me that she was afraid to speak with him because she felt as though there was something very special about him. I asked Ashley to elaborate on what she meant by that. And she advised, "For me...he's the one." I asked my beautiful, dreamy-eyed daughter, "How do you expect that he's going to be 'the one' if you are too afraid to speak with him?" And she simply giggled, while advising, "I don't know." I started laughing and made a few sarcastic jokes as far as how to go about breaking the ice with the firefighter. Although Ashley was laughing hysterically, she retorted, "Do your church friends know you talk like that?!" I sarcastically responded, "I don't know, and quite honestly I don't care." (I was secretly contemplating that I needed to find a strategy to break my daughter up with her current boyfriend, so the boy next door would have a decent chance with her.)

That being said, I know that I'm not the only parent who has experienced feelings of concern over individuals my children have chose to date. If you're a parent, you understand what I'm talking about. I'm wise enough to know that who my children marry isn't my choice, but their own. I think most parents are hopeful that once their children reach maturity, they'll get along with their daughter(s)- or son(s)-in-law. That way they can look forward to family gatherings and eventually grandchildren.

I'm not the only parent who has the ability to recognize that children have the potential to become a parent's greatest joy as well as accomplishment. Yet sometimes they are the greatest frustration and heartbreak. I know this, as I've invested a significant amount of time with each of my children, familiar with each of their goals, interests, strengths, and so on.

Parents serve a very important role in supporting the goals of their children, in order for them to be successful within this life. Unfortunately, within the breakdown of the average American family residing within the United States, as well as the breakdown of morals and virtues in our culture, not every individual would agree with my statement. Nonetheless, in order for a child to strive to achieve their maximum potential within this society, they must have a parent who morally supports their futuristic goals and ambitions in a healthy, loving, realistic, unselfish manner. As I sat there that morning, drinking coffee with my eldest child, I prayed that she would graduate from beauty college and become a successful entrepreneur within southern California as she had planned.

This conversation with my daughter was abruptly interrupted as the residential telephone rang. I stood up to answer the telephone and found my way to the home office. Ashley followed me back into the house and walked upstairs. Jacob was still playing quietly in the family room, while watching one of his favorite televised children's programs.

I answered the telephone, and it was a gentleman answering the questions I had pertaining to a new medical health insurance plan that I had previously inquired about with his office. While I was seated at my home office desk, he and I conversed over the telephone. As he spoke, I recall hearing the faint sound of countless rescue vehicles in the distance, distracting me from the telephone conversation a few times. Momentarily, I got up from where I was sitting and glanced in at Jacob very quickly. Jacob's interests at the time were rescue vehicles, specifically fire trucks. He looked up at me and smiled. I turned my attention back to the telephone conversation and sat back down in the home office.

Moments later, the neighbor's son started knocking on the front door of my home. My first thought was, "Awesome! Perhaps he is here to ask Ashley if she would like to ride his new motorcycle with him." Unfortunately, that was not the case. As I approached the doorway, I noted that the neighbor's son had his motorcycle helmet resting at the side of his waist. He appeared pale and solemn. I asked the insurance representative to hold on for a moment, so I could speak with the guest standing in my doorway. The neighbor's son started to speak, saying the following words that I will never forget for as long as I live: "Don't panic. Your daughter has been in a vehicle collision down the street." As he spoke, the first individual of whom I thought could possibly have been in a vehicle collision was Ariel, since she was carpooling with a friend's family, since I thought Ashley was still upstairs. Meanwhile, at the same time, the other line to my telephone began to alert me that there was a call waiting to be answered. Therefore, I answered the other line while inviting the neighbor's son into my home. I managed to get both individuals off of the telephone, apprising each of them that I had to address a family emergency. Once I had hung up the telephone, I gave the neighbor's son my undivided attention. Once again, while struggling to hold his composure, he proceeded to inform me that my daughter had been in a vehicle collision. The approximate location was just three blocks from home. I remember inquiring if he was sure it was Ashley. He nodded. I was sure he was wrong. To prove it, I called out to Ashley while he and I stood in the elegantly decorated foyer. When she didn't respond, it was apparent she had left the house quietly, unannounced while I had been distracted on the telephone with the health insurance representative. I was standing there in the foyer in my pajamas, staring wide-eyed at the neighbor's son. Immediately I concluded, "I need to get dressed!" He nodded. And then I asked him if he could watch over Jacob for me. He nodded in agreement. I bolted upstairs back to my bedroom and threw on a pair of sweats within a matter of seconds. I rushed back downstairs, grabbed the keys to my vehicle, and advised the neighbor's son that I'd return in a few moments. Then I drove my vehicle down to the intersection where the vehicle collision had occurred, expecting to see a minor fender bender.

There is nothing anyone could've ever said or done to prepare me for what I saw within the fraction of a second when I pulled up to that intersection. Ashley's turquoise-colored Pontiac Sunfire was crushed like an aluminum can. Immediate panic filled my being. My heart beating rapidly, in heavy turmoil, I jumped out of my vehicle, noting an undocumented number of rescue vehicles and countless bystanders, as I made my way through the crowd in the direction of Ashley's vehicle. My throat tightened as I looked to the left and the right, unable to find her amidst the wreckage of her small sports car. In that moment, I experienced what is classified to theologians as a Kyros moment, when God seemingly slows time down, when everything except the individual experiencing the *Kyros* moment is moving in slow motion, allowing the individual to register exactly everything going on within a single, miniscule fraction of time. A male police officer approached me and asked me to step away from Ashley's vehicle. I firmly responded, "Where is *my* daughter?!!!" He confirmed that I was the accident victim's mother before getting on his transmitter and advising his colleagues, "I have Jane Doe's mother here." I quickly corrected the police officer and advised, "My daughter's name is *not* 'Jane Doe'! Her name is Ashley. Now where is she?!!!" Meanwhile, I was thinking, *Don't these rescue workers know enough to check the glove compartment or an individual's wallet for identification?* The officer advised me that Ashley was next to the ambulance and that I'd probably not be able to get through the human barricade set up by the rescue workers. I left his side at once and headed in the direction of the ambulance and the human barricade they had set up. The moment I caught sight of

Ashley lying on a gurney on the ground outside of the ambulance, I tore through that barricade, in spite of their efforts to keep individuals out. I shook them off in order to kneel at my daughter's right side. She was clearly unconscious and wearing a brace that the paramedics had positioned around her neck. They had positioned a portable respirator over her nose and mouth to administer oxygen to her, while traces of both blood and tears ran down the sides of her face. I fell to my knees on the ground at her right side, with one of the paramedics also kneeling on her other side. I felt helpless, even angry, as the other paramedic advised that I wouldn't be allowed to ride in the ambulance with Ashley. I choked back my tears and sobs while I patiently and calmly advised Ashley that I wouldn't be able to ride in the ambulance with her. I reminded her that Jesus is omnipresent and that He would be accompanying her to the hospital. Then I took hold of Ashley's right hand and prayed to God out loud, while both the paramedics and I were still uncertain of the injuries that she had sustained during the catastrophic vehicle collision... the collision that quite literally changed her life as she knew it.

As the paramedic team loaded my child inside of the ambulance, an officer advised me that one of their officers would drive me to the hospital in one of the squad cars. I advised the officer that I had to return to my residence because I had a three-year-old child at home waiting for me, and I asked if they could arrange for the officer to meet with me at my residence. He said, "Yes." I believe it was they who notified my spouse, informing him that he needed to leave work and return home immediately, despite the fact I had requested a divorce from him the night before. He didn't realize the severity of the collision until later that day.

Hurriedly, I made my way back through the crowd and to my vehicle. I returned to my residence and parked my vehicle in the driveway. A female officer followed me back to my house and asked me to sit in the front side passenger seat of the squad car. I climbed into the squad car, sat down, buckled my seat belt, and waited. Meanwhile, the officer spoke with the neighbor's son who was watching over my son. She briefed him over the severity of the situation, and then asked him to watch over Jacob for a little while longer. Meanwhile my heart was pounding inside of my chest, racing, as a result of this catastrophic event.

As I sat in the squad car, suddenly I felt two invisible arms wrap around me, embracing me from behind. Then the presence rested its hand over my heart as I sat there. The being slowed my heart rate down while telepathically speaking words into my heart, "Ashley's going to survive." The heavenly messenger spoke words of life and advised me to "pray and wait" while tears of both grief and complete amazement filled my eyes. I sat there quietly and allowed the angelic being sent from heaven to comfort my spirit.

A few moments later, the officer returned to the squad car. I turned toward her and advised her, "I was just embraced by an angel. The angel said that Ashley's going to survive." The officer looked at me and didn't respond. We pulled out of the neighborhood and headed directly to the hospital where Ashley had been transported. While en route to the hospital emergency room, driving north on the I-15 freeway, I sat in the squad car in shock. I decided to make a few telephone calls from my wireless device. One of the first telephone calls I remember making was to my home church, notifying the church board committee that I had an urgent prayer request as well as a powerful testimony about my unmistakable, extraordinary encounter with a heavenly being outside of my residence, inside of a...squad car.

Once the police officer and I arrived at the hospital, the emergency room doctors met me out in the parking lot. Ashley was already stationed in a trauma room. While speaking with me outside of the hospital, the emergency room doctors appeared perplexed over the injuries Ashley had sustained as a result of the collision.

They advised me, with tears in their eyes, they didn't think she would survive throughout the evening. I encouraged each of the doctors that Ashley was going to survive, and they needed to get back in there and work to save her. They advised me that they'd do their very best and proceeded to conduct a thorough examination, ordered special tests, and even performed exploratory surgery upon my child, while one of the hospital employees showed me to an area where I could wait.

Pastor Ken (Ashley's youth pastor) and Pastor Anthony were the first to arrive and meet with me at the hospital. They had advised me that they were in a church board meeting at the time I had notified the church office by telephone of the accident. Therefore, they rose to the occasion and left the board meeting immediately upon receiving my urgent message. They sat with me and a hospital volunteer for quite some time. We prayed together. Ashley required a healing miracle, subsequently, the intervention of faith, God's mercy, as well as the precise intervention of skilled healthcare providers in order to save her life. During that time, I advised as well as encouraged every one of her doctors and surgeons that God would guide their minds and hands, to erase their doubt.

After the emergency room doctors had completed exploratory surgery, they advised that Ashley should be flown to a different hospital through means of a helicopter (aka: Life Flight). They described Ashley's injuries to me, advising me she was unconscious and their department had placed her in "a drug-induced coma" to keep her still and prevent her from moving around in the event she awakened, to avoid further trauma to her slender anatomy. Within those delicate hours, we soon learned that Ashley had sustained quite a few injuries as a result of her vehicle collision—injuries that were both devastatingly life-threatening and some that weren't. Ashley's list of injuries included but were not limited to a closed head fracture and contusions to her skull, traumatic brain injury, pupil dilation "Affixia" to one of her eyes, fractures to her neck vertebrae, injury to her brainstem, a crushed rib cage severing the aorta to her heart, collapsed lungs, a ruptured sternum, injury and contusions to her spleen and liver, fractures to her hips, and a shattered pelvic area. Her hands also had contusions, appearing as though a few of her fingers might be broken. She had countless contusions as well as lacerations from the shattered glass of her vehicle all over her small 130-pound frame. The lacerations were so deep they eventually would leave countless scars.

While we waited for the Life Flight team to arrive, I was finally allowed to visit the dimly lit hospital observation room, where Ashley had been temporarily assigned. She was resting. Yet, she appeared almost life-less, silent, in critical condition. A hospital volunteer accompanied me into the observation room. Nonethe-less I softly spoke words of life into my daughter's frag-ile being as though she were wide awake, trusting she could hear my voice. I prayed her subconscious would contemplate every word of life and love that I spoke.

Within a few moments, the Life Flight team arrived, the members of the clergy left, and the hospital admin-istrative team gave me the information as to where my daughter was being transported. By that time, my husband Jason had arrived and met up with me in the family waiting area. He apologized, not understanding the *severity* of the vehicle collision until arriving at the hospital. Before I left the hospital with him, an emer-gency room healthcare employee placed into the palm of my left hand a few pieces of jewelry: Ashley's high school graduation ring that I had purchased for her, an eyebrow ring as well as her belly button ring. The clattering sound that the stainless steel and white gold made upon falling into the palm of my hand that after-noon was almost heart-wrenching. I'll never forget that sound. Each piece of jewelry had been severed from her anatomy by the healthcare staff due to the injuries she had sustained. They explained that her jewelry had to be removed because her body had started swelling as a result of massive trauma as well as due to the emergency exploratory surgery the medical staff had to perform. The clothing she was wearing that morning, I'm guessing, was disposed of, perhaps as a result of being removed by means of scissors in order for the healthcare team to perform necessary immediate emergency medical treatment.

Jason and I left the hospital together and returned to our residence to meet up with our two other children. We hadn't notified Ariel yet to apprise her that her sister had been in a vehicle collision so as to not disrupt her school schedule. Jacob was still under the care of the neighbor's son over the course of approximately five hours, at that point.

Once we arrived at our residence, Ariel staggered out of the house grief-stricken, sobbing, advising us that a few folks had told her on the way home from school that day that Ashley had been in a vehicle collision. The roadways had been closed down for hours. They told her that her sister had died in that car crash. Whoever said to Ariel that day, that "Ashley had died in a car accident" and whatever their intentions were, couldn't have been any further from the truth. They misinformed my youngest daughter. What they said was untrue and cruel. Yet Ariel wasn't the only individual to hear that vicious rumor. While I can empathize entirely with Ariel,

I can't even imagine how she felt while walking home from school that day, especially returning home to an empty house, having received such upsetting and inaccurate news, and mourning the supposed death of her older sister, in those few moments...alone. I speculate she probably wondered where I was, where Jacob was, and if we had also been in the vehicle collision. There Ariel (who was thirteen years old at the time) sat grieving, without anyone to comfort her or answer any of her questions, until I arrived. I embraced Ariel immediately. She was so distraught. I advised her that her sister had indeed been in a catastrophic vehicle collision. However, I informed her that Ashley was still very much alive...although she was in very fragile condition. I advised her that her sister was being Life-Flighted to a hospital south of the township we resided in and that I needed her to get ready to leave in route to the hospital with us.

A distraught Ariel hesitated, almost in disbelief. So, I advised her, "If you want me to prove to you that Ashley's still very much alive, please get ready to leave." Ariel instantaneously gathered a few belongings and prepared to visit the hospital. Within a few moments, my small family began the 90-minute trip straight to the hospital where Ashley was transported that day and immediately admitted into the Trauma Ward.

The Word of God promises to comfort those who experience great sorrow:

"God blesses those who mourn, for they will be comforted."
—Matthew 5:4 NLT

2

The Battle for Life

"I'm hanging on to the promises of God."

—Wendy Adams

My husband drove while we were in route to the hospital. I made a few telephone calls from my wireless telephone from the front-side passenger seat. I remember looking over at him at one point and saying, "Could you please drive a little faster? It feels as though we're moving at about 25 mph." He advised me that he was driving a little faster than the posted speed limit on the southern California freeway, and he refused to drive any faster. I was sitting there staring at him for a few moments thinking, *I should've driven*, because I was sure he wasn't driving anywhere close to the posted speed limit. Momentarily, I leaned over and glanced down at the MPH gauge and looked at him again, and sort of let out a sigh of discord. I decided to turn my attention back to my wireless telephone and busied myself with notifying relatives. Meanwhile, Jacob sat in his car seat in the second row of the vehicle, next to his sister Ariel, both quiet. About an hour later, my husband, our two youngest children, and I arrived at the southern California hospital. Ashley had already arrived. We were asked to take a seat in the family waiting area on the same floor.

Meanwhile health care providers scrambled to stabilize Ashley, while family, church family, friends, Ashley's college classmates, and their family members slowly showed up at the hospital to visit, pray, and wait with us. We had the front seat to an incredibly long wait during a time of great uncertainty. The medical team didn't believe Ashley would survive the night.

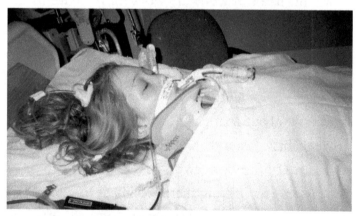

Ashley's post-accident photo, 2004.

After speaking with the doctors, I was overwhelmed with Ashley's extensive number of life-threatening injuries, unsure if she'd survive. She was in "SEVERE critical condition"—near death. Yet she was still alive. Praise God! Therefore, while the trauma team tried to get Ashley stabilized in the operating room, I multitasked, tending to my two other children, answering numerous questions from health care providers and other hospital staff, completing medical history forms, signing consent forms, and speaking with police officers. Our family was *inundated* with an undocumented number of visitors as well as telephone callers, frequently requesting an update on Ashley's prognosis. Each individual experienced feelings of both grief and helplessness over the situation. I patiently spoke with each of the individuals, praying with some of them. Yet I was also attentive to answer each of their questions and listen to Ashley's friends recite their personal stories and favorite memories of my daughter. Many individuals who showed up at the hospital chose to wait in the designated waiting area, while others formed a line within the hospital corridor. Each individual was mourning the gruesome reality of Ashley's vehicle collision, requiring encouragement and patiently waiting to visit with her...even for a few short moments.

That day, Jason assisted with watching over my rambunctious son and being cordial with the visitors. Once the trauma team allowed Ashley to have visitors,

I escorted Ariel *first* into the room, so she could see her sister. Ashley was indeed alive, breathing by means of life support equipment, but she was comatose. Multiple medical tubes and wires extended from Ashley's anatomy, monitoring her vitals; administering medications, fluids, and oxygen; draining her lungs of fluid; etc., as she lay unconscious. As I stood there staring at Ashley in alarm, noticing her external injuries, being aware of her internal injuries, and noting her vitals were all triple digits, I observed her countenance looked like a peaceful, sleeping beauty as though she wasn't experiencing any pain at all but only resting. Yet, all I could think was, *My eldest baby has been hurt, and I can't even hold her in my arms.* Meanwhile, my second-born child stood there, stared at her older sister, and sobbed, while trying to speak to Ashley. I attempted to comfort Ariel before exiting the room and returning to the waiting room down the hallway. The hospital wouldn't allow more than two or three guests at a time in the room Ashley had been assigned to, and they only permitted ten to fifteen minutes per visitor. What's more, according to hospital policy, no one other than health care personnel were allowed to touch Ashley. Relatives weren't even allowed to hold her hand, due to the trauma her body had sustained. Therefore, we prayed a lot that day.

Eventually, Jason decided to return home with my two youngest children, and he left me at the hospital to stay with Ashley.

In the early days of Ashley's hospitalization, at the age of thirty-five, I was appointed her sole advocate and legal guardian, having to make countless difficult decisions along with her doctors, pertaining to her life while she was comatose. She was eighteen years of age, but she was unconscious and incapable of making decisions for herself. Each consent form clearly advised me of the "Risks and Benefits" associated with the various medical procedures that were *necessary* to perform with the sole intent to save her life. There was a high level of pressure in making such decisions. It was so intense that I prayed and then I would anoint each consent form with anointing oil before providing my signature. The decisions I had to make in reference to Ashley's life were complicated, to say the least. I experienced a lot of pressure and felt I was placed in a position to play the role of God within my own child's life. Nothing in my upbringing, education, training, or professional experience had ever prepared me for that moment. I was truly scared for the first time in my life, completely aware that her fate depended on my signature and reasoning. After signing such consent forms, often times, I'd leave the trauma ward and visit the prayer room located on a different floor of the hospital to pray, pleading with Jesus for intercessory prayer.

I was preoccupied for countless hours at Ashley's side, praying for her as her vitals were frighteningly elevated. I was perplexed during each step of her medical case. She was on life support equipment and she required forty units of blood in less than a week after being hospitalized. The deafening sound of alarms from Ashley's life support equipment and other medical machinery frequently filled the environment of her small quiet hospital room, alerting the health care providers that she required their immediate attention. In those moments, I shuddered with fear, wondering whether or not Ashley was about to graduate to heaven. Yet, I was fully aware I wasn't emotionally prepared to let her go. Oftentimes, I asked God during prayer if I was making the right decisions for her. Quite literally this horrific event in Ashley's life shook me to the very foundation of my faith and reduced me to my knees. I needed reassurance my child was going to survive. I needed someone to confirm that my angelic encounter wasn't my "imagination." Yet, instead, I was presented with individuals looking to me for encouragement as well as answers. I was fortunate for members of the clergy who showed up on the scene.

Then suddenly, the Holy Spirit placed it on my heart to provide a guestbook for Ashley's visitors to sign. The guestbook would eventually be positioned on a table at the foot of her hospital bed for relatives, friends, other visitors, and health care personnel to sign to leave their well wishes. One wall of Ashley's hospital room was adorned with an array of greeting cards, as well as a single George W. Bush presidential campaign sticker, a sticker that happened to somehow escape the stack that Ashley was holding on the morning of October 11, 2004. During Ashley's hospitalization, I happened to find said campaign sticker wedged between the front seat and the console of my vehicle and I had to laugh, recalling that day very well. So, I decided to bring the campaign sticker to Ashley's hospital room and affix it somewhere she could see it, in the event she awakened from the coma. Miraculously, George W. Bush ended up being elected president that year.

Meanwhile, on the home front, my family advised me that my residential telephone was ringing off the hook. While many individuals visited to bring gifts, cards, and food to assist us during our time of grief, one church youth group was kind enough to invite Ariel to attend services at their church, in order to pray with her and provide her with moral support while I was busy at the hospital tending to her sister, her stepdad was busy with his employment obligations, and her brother was at Christian preschool.

Several days after Ashley's vehicle collision, one of the police officers assigned to the case notified me on the hospital telephone to advise that their department was in the middle of conducting an investigation pertaining to the accident. Ashley's vehicle had been removed from the accident scene and towed to an area where their team of investigators could conduct their investigation, until further notice. Essentially, no one other than their department was allowed access to the vehicle. The officer also advised me that the other driver involved in the collision wished to speak with me.

Our family wasn't acquainted with the other driver. We had no knowledge as to whether the other driver was "under the influence" at the time of the collision or if he was deliberately driving recklessly or not. We didn't even know whether or not he had a medical condition to be concerned with. All we knew, at that point, was that he was in his late sixties and that he didn't apply his brakes after broadsiding Ashley's sports car. His response to the accident was relatively unusual, according to one witness, while his story to the police department was entirely different. The other driver falsely accused Ashley of being on a cellular telephone at the time of the collision, implying that it was she who was driving inattentively. I advised the investigator of the police department that "Ashley didn't own a wireless telephone" and told him that "the other driver was obviously telling their department a bold-faced lie." They recorded my response as a part of their investigation.

What's more, I was made aware from one witness, a Christian man, at the scene of the accident that the other driver had stated that Ashley "deserved to be hit," while he also made a fair attempt to discourage the witness from notifying 911. Fortunately, the witness ignored the other driver, while wasting no time to notify rescue services and then proceeded to pray with a still very alert Ashley. The witness advised me that while he approached Ashley's vehicle, "she was crying, appearing to be drowning on her own blood, while trapped inside of the crushed vehicle." The witness continued, "Once I prayed with her and said, 'Amen,' Ashley went unconscious, slumped forward, and blood gushed from both her mouth and nose." The witness stayed at her side until rescue workers arrived. Two officers literally had to physically pull the door off of Ashley and extract her from the wreckage of the vehicle. Her driver's-side bucket seat was sandwiched between the front passenger seat and the backseat of the sports car, with the seat belt still attached around her body, which had somehow contributed to cutting off her airway, unfortunately. The witness concluded that he too was experiencing symptoms of post-traumatic stress disorder as a result of what he had witnessed after the vehicle collision. He assured me that he had given his testimony to the police department before he had called me.

That being said, at the time the police officer notified me at the hospital during a different conversation, I announced that I had pondered how the other driver was coping since the day of the collision. I advised the officer that I had prayed for him, while also praying for my daughter, as I had knowledge that in the event Ashley didn't survive, the other driver would be faced with charges of involuntary manslaughter and possibly do time in prison as a result. The officer asked if I would accept a telephone call from the individual who had broadsided my daughter's vehicle. I said, "Yes."

Upon the other driver notifying me telephonically at the hospital, I was very patient and polite toward him. I asked him how he was doing. Initially he advised that he was experiencing an overwhelming amount of personal anguish since the day of the collision. He, too, had been informed that Ashley had not survived. Evidently, after the collision, he had been given the same inaccurate story pertaining to Ashley's prognosis as my daughter Ariel had been given and he was also grieving, until he'd noted Ashley's story in the local newspaper, which prompted him to want to speak with me. I invited the other driver to the hospital, so that way I could meet with him in person and have the opportunity to pray with him. While he expressed his relief that Ashley was still alive, he refused to meet with me in person. I never heard from the other driver again after that day. However, neither do I harbor ill will against him.

I'm uncertain who was responsible for putting misleading information into circulation pertaining to Ashley's prognosis on the day of the collision. However, what I know is such an inaccurate account deeply distressed both my daughter Ariel as well as the other driver.

During a conversation, an officer articulated a mannequin head had fallen out of the vehicle trunk, from Ashley's cosmetology duffel bag, upon the other driver impacting Ashley's sports car. All but one police officer was apprehensive to approach the mannequin head, believing that someone had been decapitated during the accident. A female officer rose to the occasion and walked over to the mannequin head, leaned over, and picked it up from the roadside. Then, while holding it in her grasp, she looked at her colleagues and assured them that it was a fake head. One can imagine the relief of the group of police officers standing there in the distance upon learning of this, as well as the razzing amongst colleagues once they returned to their office. This was one of several conversations communicated to me from the police department while Ashley was in critical condition.

While both true and untrue stories took off like wildfire, eventually Ashley's biological father, Kevin, a man whom I had once been engaged to but never married, made it to the hospital. He had temporarily left his family, having traveled in from the Midwest, and he'd somehow gotten off on the wrong flight at an airport north of San Diego, California. He claimed he had walked as well as hitchhiked from an airport located in northern California.

Immediately, Kevin and I had conflicting interests with regard to our daughter's life, as well as arguments pertaining to our own personal religious views. He demanded that I have Ashley's life support equipment "unplugged." He'd make his unwelcome remarks on a few occasions over something pertaining to his concern over her future "quality of life." Needless to say, I refused to concede to Kevin's requests and asked that he kindly refrain from his blasphemic comments, pertaining to his thoughts about God, considering the circumstances.

There were moments when the trauma team would get Ashley "stable," and moments later, things would change within a matter of seconds...regression as opposed to progress, without notice. The alarms from the medical equipment sounding off were nerve-racking. In my heart, I wanted to hold on to hope and be optimistic, despite the fact that internally my spirit was flailing in despair over my child. I so wanted to hold on to the promise from my heavenly messenger on October 12, 2004, over the subject of being advised Ashley would survive. However, I was becoming weary from lack of rest and hearing so much negativity from others. I longed to be home with my family. Yet, I didn't want to leave Ashley's side in the event she either awakened or passed away.

Neurologist specialists advised me that Ashley, at the time, had "little to no brain activity." I pondered whether Ashley's subconscious could hear everything going on or being said around her, and I wondered if the conversations as well as the alarms were upsetting her. I prayed after the nurse relayed what the neurology department had said. After praying, I notified Dawn, a dear church friend of mine. We used to sing in the choir together on Sunday mornings at our home church, in the alto section. I asked her if she could bring a few Christian music CDs as well as a portable music CD player with earphones. Immediately, she said, "Yes," and she delivered the items to the hospital. We prayed together. Eventually her husband, a USN military veteran as well as a minister, also visited. I then placed the earphones on Ashley and started playing Christian music for her to listen to while in the level 0 coma.

I also speculated that in the event she awakened suddenly, and I happened to not be present, she'd know I wasn't too far away. Ashley used to refer to Christian music as "Mom's music." I'm glad to advise that implementing Christian music quite literally started to stimulate Ashley's brain activity within a matter of days. That in itself was one of those "YAY!!! Team JESUS!" moments, for sure.

3

Hold On

In Ashley's hospital room, I busied myself with gloved hands and a set of stainless-steel, needle-nosed, cotton pliers, as a nurse and I took turns picking countless fragments of broken glass out of my daughter's scalp. We noticed the overwhelming number of deep flesh wounds caused from said fragments. Eventually we were successful at removing all of the shards of glass. We then devised a plan to wash Ashley's hair with a plastic cup and an unused plastic bedpan (used as a basin to catch the water) to enable us to wash the dried blood from her scalp and out of the strands of her long hair while she lay in her hospital bed. We were successful at washing her hair. However, we had to be extremely gentle due to her neck injury as well as the extent of her other life-threatening injuries, as tubing was positioned in Ashley's small mouth and nostrils, literally administering oxygen to her frail being, connected to a machine that sat at her bedside doing all the breathing for her. Tubing had been surgically placed in each side of her rib area in order to drain the mixture of blood and water from her lungs, and it all led to plastic containers below her bedside. There were moments when I sat there staring in horror at the containers, feeling nauseated and faint, watching those containers fill an undocumented number of times with said fluid, completely aware I was staring at containers full of my own daughter's blood.

There was the unmistakable scent of infection in the air within that small trauma ward hospital room. I noticed smaller tubes intravenously administering necessary fluids to keep her hydrated, as well as an array of medications to heal infection and reduce physical pain. A feeding tube was placed inside of her abdomen to nourish her with formula.

Over the course of a few days, I lost track of both the time and the date, sitting in the corner of that dimly lit room. That's where my mother found me upon arriving at the hospital with an overnight bag in tow, packed with a fresh change of clothes, hygiene supplies, and other items. She took one look at me and said, "You need a shower and some rest." And I responded, "No, I don't." I stared at my mother, while she stood in the doorway of that room. She knew I was grieving. I swallowed my tears, while my innermost being needed her to say something that would be of encouragement.

I didn't want to leave my daughter's side. My mother repeated herself, "You need a shower, some rest and something to eat." I retorted, "No, I don't." Eventually, that day, my mother was successful at persuading me away from the corner of that room that I had diligently stationed myself in.

After a few nights, my two youngest children and husband picked me up from the hospital. We had dinner at a nearby Chinese restaurant. We all were sort of solemn. However, after our meal, we opened our fortune cookies. I saved mine and opened it in the vehicle. Once again, God had a short, subtle, encouraging reminder exclusively for our family, as the message from my fortune cookie read, "You will soon witness a miracle." I glanced over from the passenger front seat and in the direction of my husband behind the driver's wheel, then to each of my youngest children seated in the second row of the vehicle. I read the message out loud with tears of joy in my eyes. I saved that inspirational message and eventually placed it inside of Ashley's scrapbook.

What I know about God is that *everything* in the world and throughout the entire galaxy actually belongs to Him. Therefore, moments such as that don't happen by mere coincidence. God finds any means possible to reach His children, to speak with them, especially during times of great suffering. That message received from that single fortune cookie that day I'm certain was God's way of not only encouraging us, but also confirming the angelic messenger's communication as well as the encounter with me on the day of Ashley's collision. My reaction and thoughts were, *Awesome, I have divine favor. God is now communicating with me through this small piece of paper, tucked inside of an Asian cookie.*

As I recall such events, it was as if God and I were engaged in a magnificent, super-secret with one another, and it was hard to keep it to myself, as I struggled silently with intermittent doubts of the unknown. I wondered if anyone in this world would ever believe my testimony. Yet, I didn't want to contain it. However, I wanted to protect my testimony from those, whether believers or unbelievers, who would dare taint such miraculous moments with their disparaging, unwelcome remarks about my angelic encounter. I prayed relentlessly; a healing miracle for Ashley truly was on its way.

After we left the restaurant, I finally had some alone time with my husband. He wept in my arms after having seen Ashley on life support equipment. He seemed to have experienced an abrupt awakening on how very fragile life is, and he discovered a newfound appreciation for his family and stepchild. That night, he profusely apologized for how difficult he had been before Ashley's vehicle collision. At that point, we mutually agreed to postpone our plans of separating/divorcing one another and hold fast to our vows, while I addressed urgent matters at the hospital.

The closed head injury Ashley had sustained to her brain during the vehicle collision started to swell, and the intracranial pressure (ICP) couldn't be controlled by means of medication, Mannitol, any longer. ICP levels aren't supposed to go beyond 20. However, Ashley's ICP level had reached an alarming 35. Therefore, one evening, after I had left the hospital, I received an urgent telephone call in the middle of the night. The trauma team was advising that they needed me to return to the hospital to sign a consent form, as it was necessary for the surgeons to place a shunt within the top of Ashley's skull to relieve the intracranial pressure. Fortunately, I was only a few blocks away, sleeping in a motel room, having just fallen to sleep, and then receiving that urgent telephone call. Therefore, I was able to get back over to the hospital right away.

After the shunt placement, I noted they had shaved one section of my daughter's head, the access point, for the procedure. One of the nurses handed me the loose strands of Ashley's hair after I entered the hospital room. Traces of Ashley's blood were still within the locks of hair, placed inside of a clear plastic bag that they gave to me.

That evening, after I returned to my residence, and after my two youngest children were tucked in for bed, I went to sit in the garage alone for a while with our family pet dog, Bingo. It was then that I started sobbing, while holding that plastic bag of Ashley's blond hair in my grasp. Bingo sat there staring at me while I wept for the first time since the day of Ashley's collision. I guessed Bingo was cognizant something was wrong, considering how infrequently I was home during the day. Ashley was also not home and the sudden increase of visitors at the residence likely confused him. I decided to speak to Bingo as I sat there. I advised him what had happened to Ashley and allowed him to sniff a lock of her hair for a moment. He listened intently, resting his head on my knee as though sulking, understanding and perplexed over my anguish, while I proceeded to weep.

4

Faith

On the morning of Saturday, October 23, 2004, the day of Ashley's aorta surgery, I anxiously, yet gladly, assisted with the preliminary preparations before the surgical procedure. While preparing Ashley for a bed bath before surgery, I noticed the area from her sternum to her pelvic area was adorned with a series of metal staples, neatly covered in an elongated medical dressing that resembled a zipper, It was a result of the exploratory surgery. It looked incredibly painful, and I was very empathetic. Once Ashley was taken to the operating area, both emotions and tension were high that day for both the family as well as for the cardiovascular surgeons.

We did not know whether or not Ashley would survive the surgery, as she was still in very fragile, "critical condition." Therefore, before she was taken off to the operating room, I had the wonderful opportunity to pray with her, as well as with one of the cardiovascular surgeons.

While Ashley was in surgery, I waited down the hallway, alone, apart from those seated in the family waiting area, finding a chair to sit down on in the lobby of that floor that lead to the trauma department. I wanted to be alone. Internally, I was flailing emotionally, coping with the greatest pain I had ever experienced since becoming a mother. I was sleep-deprived and stressed out, while contending with feelings of relentless anguish as well as anxiety with regard to the magnitude of Ashley's medical case and injuries. I attempted to ignore my emotions while praying, journaling, and trying to be optimistic for my family.

I had skipped meals for several days, and I ended up collapsing while Ashley was in surgery. I think I collapsed as a result of a combination of factors: stress overload, over-exhaustion, and my right leg had temporarily fallen asleep (gone numb), perhaps as a result of the position I was sitting while waiting in the hospital corridor. I had opted to sit away from the others waiting in the designated waiting area during Ashley's surgery. I dropped to the floor suddenly, but with grace, according to the hospital visitors who scrambled from where they were standing in order to pick me up from the tiled floor. They placed me in a wheelchair, and one person intervened to get the attention of nearby health care personnel while another went to go find my mother in the waiting room. The third individual stayed with me. I was fortunate that I hadn't hit my head. It was clear, however, that I had sprained and bruised my ankle very badly as a result of falling.

As I sat in the hallway in a wheelchair, waiting for ice packs from the health care personnel to apply to my sprained ankle, within a few moments I heard the sound of seething rhetoric from my mother echoing from the opposite end of the hallway, the very moment she turned the corner and saw me sitting there. Yes. My mother decided to harangue me.

I innocently smiled back at her and responded, while in a sort of catatonic state, "Mom, my daughter is having open heart surgery right now." My mother reassured, "Yes, I know." Then as I stared at my mother, I felt my countenance change into that of desperation as I fought back tears and searched my mother's face for any encouragement that Ashley would survive the surgery. Moments later, she sent me away to get something to eat in the hospital cafeteria, even though I didn't feel hungry. I sported my wireless telephone, the Holy Bible and my journal close at my side. Ashley's dad, Kevin, decided to take the initiative to push the wheelchair that I was sitting in, also seemingly wanting to get away from the massive crowd of visitors for a few moments. Meanwhile, I was thinking, *Where is my husband?* He hadn't arrived at the hospital yet that day.

After visiting the hospital cafeteria, Ashley's dad and I went outside, where I noticed banners advertising that there was a cardio convention scheduled within San Diego, California. Thus, advising cardio surgeons from around the world would be congregating in southern California for said convention. Then Ashley's dad and I returned inside of the hospital and joined the others waiting in the designated waiting area. Sometime after we returned, joining the others within the waiting room, my husband finally made an appearance and took his seat next to me.

Ashley had been in the operating room for an estimated eight-hour period, requiring ten additional units of blood during her surgery, while several surgeons repaired the aorta to Ashley's heart, by placing a Dacron mesh material around the laceration and then repairing a few of her ribs during the surgery as well.

"Your daughter has two things working in her favor; her age as well as her mother's faith."

–A UCSD Cardiovascular Surgeon
in San Diego County, CA

While looking gaunt, as well as in pure awe, the cardiovascular surgeon advised us that the surgery was a success and that Ashley was now in stable condition. He then proceeded to describe, in front of a room full of intently listening family members, friends, and other witnesses what he and his colleagues witnessed during Ashley's surgery, something that was mind-staggering in comparison to what they knew from their medical textbooks and experience. The cardio surgeon advised us that the aorta had been held together by a few strands where the laceration was located and a fine layer of blood clot had formed around the laceration, serving as a sort of temporary bandage, contributing to temporarily closing off the laceration located on the aorta and reducing internal bleeding. He said he and his colleagues had never encountered anything like this before. However, they were astounded as well as grateful. Therefore, with great humility, I advised the cardio surgeon that what he and his colleagues had witnessed during Ashley's surgery was a "miracle." I told them, "It was as though God's own hand was holding things together in her chest until you guys could get in there and perform the procedure." The doctor concurred. And then he announced in front of those present in the waiting room, while staring at me, "Your daughter has two things working in her favor: her age as well as her mother's faith."

He then asked me if I'd sign a consent form, granting permission for him and his colleagues to implement Ashley's cardiovascular surgical miracle story during their cardio convention lecture for the purpose of cardiovascular research as well as advancement. I gladly signed the form.

We were all so relieved that Ashley's surgery was successful and thankful that God had appointed such skilled cardio surgeons to her medical case that day as well as for His answering our persistent prayers. I was thankful to also have a few prayer warriors from my home church present.

After the doctor left the room, my mother sitting beside me, said, "I have no idea what they've been teaching you at the church that you attend. However, someday, I'm hopeful to be a strong Christian like you." While my mother's well-intended words were kind and thoughtful, during a time when our family was rejoicing over the success of Ashley's aorta surgery, I humbly advised her, "The strength I have as a believer is because of the power of Jesus Christ, and certainly not of my own strength alone." That promise of several promises is there for every individual who chooses to become a member of the Christian faith. What's more, Jesus' promise to those who are afflicted is that His strength is made perfect in weakness (2 Corinthians 12:9).

Approximately a week later, Ashley's eyes slightly started to open as though she was trying to peek beyond her eyelids and trying to awaken. She'd yawn, and on a few occasions, her hands and shoulders would move faintly. She was at a point where relatives and friends could hold her hand while they were praying. She could receive light massages, with moisturizer, to help with circulation and to aid with decreasing her hypertension.

As the weeks passed, I met a number of other families who had loved ones in the hospital. They shared in the responsibility and took shifts with one another, so the entire responsibility wasn't delegated to only one individual. They were families behaving like family should. I spent countless hours at the hospital next to Ashley's side. I recall those days more than she does, as I was awake observing, for an undocumented amount of time.

On one occasion, a trauma specialist smiled and advised me that he noted that I pulled longer shifts than anyone else did. He advised me that in the event I decided to enroll in med school, he would be more than happy to confirm my internship hours.

I expressed to their medical team that I felt helpless over Ashley's condition and that I wanted to be more useful during the time I spent within their department. Therefore, the hospital's trauma ward department decided to give me a crash course in basic medical nurses' training, considering they were a highly accredited learning hospital within the United States.

Well-meaning hospital visitors continued to travel in locally and from afar, wishing to see Ashley and wanting to speak with my family, while other folks thoughtlessly consumed the minutes of my wireless telephone, leaving countless messages throughout the day. At the time, many folks didn't realize I was trying to keep my telephone lines free, solely for immediate family (such as my spouse and children), as well as for health care personnel, in the event they needed to reach me, over an urgent matter pertaining to Ashley. There wasn't wireless reception on certain floors within the hospital. And I didn't have the time, nor the patience, to listen to a multitude of telephonic messages outside of the hospital, and I certainly did not have the interest in having an hour-long conversation with each caller. This went on for several weeks and then months. Few individuals had regard that I needed to take a break to nourish myself, rest, and tend to my other children, also.

Finally, I asked my older sister Lisa if she could intervene and respond to the overwhelming number of telephone calls that were inundating my wireless device as well as my residence. Within a short period of time, Lisa was also overwhelmed with the flood of telephone calls and messages in such a way she could hardly believe it. Therefore, she and a website designer took the initiative to create/monitor a website on behalf of Ashley, to direct individuals to a website for updates pertaining to Ashley's prognosis as an alternative resource for information. The intent was to eliminate the distraction of annoying as well as unnecessary telephone calls to the hospital nurses' desk, our wireless devices, as well as our residences.

The initial creation of the website was extremely helpful during that time, decreasing the number of telephone calls, and it was equally helpful to those who were incapable of visiting. The website designer was mindful to implement photographs and a place for online visitors to leave an online message of well wishes, a word of encouragement, or simply a prayer. The website was even designed to accurately record the frequency of visitors.

At first, the website was a blessing—especially after I was presented with a $6,000 wireless telephone bill, which my spouse, at the time, wasn't very happy about.

However, once the wireless company learned of Ashley's accident, their offices were kind enough to waive an estimated $4,000 from the enormously high debt, much to my surprise. Meanwhile, the story pertaining to Ashley's vehicle collision took off like wildfire, and like a thief metaphorically stole as well as broke the hearts of countless individuals: family members, friends, classmates, neighbors, acquaintances, health care personnel, and so forth, throughout the world, some to the extent of speechlessness. Ashley's website recorded over 35,000 hits within a short period of time. Tentatively, I don't recall what the exact number of internet visitors were by the time the website was finally shut down. However, if I remember correctly, the website received around thirty-five to forty visitors a day, over the course of about four years.

5

Complete Disarray

Eventually, Ashley's vehicle was released from the police department's investigation unit. They advised that most of Ashley's belongings had been already removed from the police department, and they had even been attentive to dry out photographs found within her purse, as after the collision and amidst their investigation, southern California was struck with thunder and lightning storms as well as rain showers. Their office was kind enough to return the items they had retrieved from her vehicle. However, they allowed me to visit the tow yard the vehicle had been transported to in order to collect any remaining personal belongings of Ashley's, as well as to take pictures of the vehicle. Among the contents returned to me was also a magnetic turquoise blue butterfly that I had purchased for Ashley and placed on the driver's side of her vehicle to surprise her, a few days before her collision. That butterfly seemed to be the only thing that went unscathed, much to my surprise.

The inside of the cabin of the now-abandoned sports car was in complete disarray; the driver's-side front seat was still sandwiched between the backseat and the passenger front seat. The remaining part of the driver's-side seat belt, severed by a police officer during the rescue, casually rested on the driver's seat. Fragments of broken plastic, glass, and other debris were scattered everywhere, along with noticeable traces of Ashley's blood dried on the fragments of glass, the upholstery, and the inside cabin of the vehicle. I practiced great caution while collecting any items that I found, so as not to injure myself, and I was careful to place items found within plastic storage bags. Within the wreckage I found Ashley's college notebook with an adhesive sticker that she had placed on the cover, to proclaim to her group of peers, "My mommy thinks I'm special." I smiled, yet I was reduced to tears in that moment. I thought, *Uh-huh, kiddo. I think you are very special.* Eventually, the adhesive sticker adorning that message was implemented within a scrapbook that I put together for her.

While examining the extent of the damages, I noted the airbags of the vehicle had failed to deploy upon impact. I wondered how fast the other vehicle was moving at the time of the collision. I notified the attorney whom I had hired and consented to a forensic specialist conducting a separate investigation, once the insurance companies also had an opportunity to examine the extent of the damages to the vehicle. Ashley's sportscar was, in a word, *totaled*.

The wreckage of Ashley's sports car.

6

Prayer Warriors

There were moments when I could be found not in Ashley's hospital room but on a different level, on my knees, my head bowed in prayer, at the altar of the prayer room located within the hospital, summoning the intervention of Jesus Himself for healing throughout my daughter's recovery, and offering prayers of comfort and strength for the rest of the family. Whether standing, leaning, sitting, or resting, I am always a soldier for the Kingdom of Jesus Christ. I know I'm a valiant warrior, having persevered and survived many battles. However, *this* particular event in Ashley's life shook my faith to the very core of my being, testing almost every aspect of my life, along with every ounce of hope I had, beyond comprehension.

Emotionally, I felt like I was swimming in the metaphoric deep sea of personal anguish, searching for a lifeboat, while waves crashed all around. The devastation was like I had never imagined nor expected to ever have to cope with after becoming a mother. I wanted absolute answers to the numerous amounts of questions troubling me. Unfortunately, there were no absolute answers from medical textbooks or from the countless highly skilled health care providers pertaining to Ashley, to my avail. There were only educated guesses and theories. Therefore, I needed Jesus to quiet the storm within, while my spirit, like a child, pleaded in desperation, "Daddy, pleeeeeease! Please allow Ashley to live!"

God is the Creator of mankind. He's the *Physician* of all physicians. Aware of each molecule and each cell within an individual's anatomy, from the top of their head to the very soles of their feet, God is conscious of the care an individual needs. That being said, while Ashley was comatose, God was watchful over Ashley. However, He was watchful over me also. I thank God that He responded wonderfully to my prayers, gracing me with other prayer warriors, wonderful members of the clergy who weren't as distraught as me. Many of them not only prayed with Ashley but also offered words of encouragement for the rest of us. Other believers would show up on the scene to sing praise and worship music within Ashley's room. Having their presence there helped me feel more at ease.

They respectfully spoke words of life, love, and hope specifically to this weary soul, as well as to Ashley. They weren't there to create conflict, to annoy, to insult, or to draw my attention away from the purpose as to why I spent so much time out at the hospital. They weren't there behaving as though they were attending a funeral ceremony, and neither were they speaking words of death.

My church family didn't place unrealistic expectations on me or any demands. Thus is why there was a point at which I stepped into the designated waiting area of the hospital and assertively said to the other guests congregating there, "If you're not here to pray...I need you all to leave. Ashley needs me more than any of you do right now."

I didn't mean to sound crass. However, there were other families there who also had a loved one in the hospital and seating was limited. Initially, I didn't want to contend with the conflict over Ashley's visitors loitering around the hospital as though they were at a coffeehouse or in the family room of my residence, at the time. I know many of them were well-meaning. Yet, I speculated at no point did they consider what they were doing, and oftentimes they overstayed their visit. After all, our family had experienced a very horrific event that we were trying to address. During the earliest days of Ashley's hospitalization, it was crucial to have positive energy encompassing her as well as myself. I was also grateful over the enormous number of Christians employed at the hospital(s) that were assigned to Ashley's care. Oftentimes they too also offered words of encouragement, instruction, and mentoring.

While I was present, I'd often read to Ashley, usually articles from a magazine, the daily newspaper, or from the Holy Bible. I'd also speak with Ashley as though she were alert, praying she could hear my voice. I pondered if she could hear me, if she was communing with Jesus Christ as well as angels, or if she was lying there in complete darkness, oblivious to everything going on around her. I prayed she was indeed communing with Jesus Christ.

I was relieved to learn from a nurse that Ashley's vitals conveyed that she felt more at ease while I was present. That nurse encouraged me to keep communicating. However, the medical team noted that Ashley's vitals would elevate after I'd leave the hospital room. Therefore, that was confirmation enough for both the nurse and me that Ashley had an awareness of her surroundings, while she was in a coma. The nurse asked if I could record my voice, so their staff could play the recordings to assist with comforting Ashley while I was away from the hospital.

Some of Ashley's friends and other relatives would host a bedside sock-puppet show alongside of me, with Ashley's collection of character socks, waiting for any form of response. On one occasion, a hospital visitor musingly said, "Someday, Ashley is going to awaken from her coma and tell you to 'Shut up!'" I laughed and went back to tending to my business, hopeful that Ashley would eventually awaken and start a conversation with me. It didn't matter to me what she said. I just longed to see her wake up and hear her voice. However, at least, we kept the hospital staff employees and med students very well entertained. They disclosed, "Each day, while the doctors make their rounds, they look forward to seeing what socks adorn Ashley's feet, completely amused." So, upon learning of this, it only encouraged us to purchase more character socks for Ashley, with the intent to entertain the doctors as well as ourselves, I suppose.

"Laughter is good medicine."
—Proverbs 17:22

About three weeks after Ashley's collision, I spoke with the manager of the gas station close to where the accident had occurred. She informed me, "The day of your daughter's collision, one of my male colleagues and I had decided to bring beverages to the rescue workers. We were already present at the time you showed up on the scene. We watched you tear through that human barricade to access your daughter. In amazement, my colleague said, 'Did you see that?!!! *That* was like...' He paused for a moment and then made reference to a su-perhero. The gas station manager and I sort of stood there laughing while contemplating that her colleague was some sort of superhero comic-book story buff." I thought, *Since I was a small child, I've enjoyed shows and movies about superheroes.* Then I switched the subject and proceeded to give the store manager a brief update on how Ashley was doing at the hospital.

Halloween

On the afternoon of October 31, 2004, Lisa appeared from the hospital parking lot dressed as an angel. She smirked while advising she had left work to spend her lunch break at the hospital with me. Once she got closer to where I was sitting, she exclaimed in an obnoxious-sounding voice, "I'm an Ashley angel!" In that moment, I clearly was not amused. My sense of humor had es-caped me as a result of REAL stress and sleep depriva-tion. Therefore, I was irritated with my sister as I sat there staring at her, trying to assess if whether or not she trying to mock me. We sat there outside of the hos-pital conversing for a few moments before she then made her way through the hospital lobby doors, to the elevators, and straight up to Ashley's hospital room. Once I also returned to the hospital room, I captured a single image with my camera of my sister dressed as an angel standing at the bedside of my eldest daughter. Eventually, I incorporated that snapshot into Ashley's scrapbook.

In early November 2004, wouldn't you know, George W. Bush was reelected as president of the United States, for a second term. Our family was happy to learn he was reelected.

Meanwhile, Ashley, still in "critical condition," was making progress, in such a manner the doctors overseeing her care implemented "sprinting"—which means the medical team had started to turn off the respiratory equipment for a few moments each day to allow Ashley to breathe on her own with little assistance from a ventilator. At first, Ashley had difficulty with this exercise; learning to breathe on her own again. I'm guessing due to the fact she had sustained a fractured rib cage and collapsed lungs as a result of the collision, and the medical treatment that followed, shortly thereafter, in order to save her life had also weakened her condition.

She started physical therapy. Those days were agonizing for me, as Ashley's hospitalization was for an indefinite time. We didn't know how long she would be in the hospital, if she would ever pull out of coma, and/ or if she would ever be strong enough to return home.

Amidst trying to juggle time between hospital visits, visitors, as well as life at home, I addressed business matters...one being an application for medical assistance on behalf of my daughter. The medical insurance I had for her had expired upon her graduating from high school, earlier that year. Before her collision, I was in the middle of trying to have her coverage "reactivated," advising their offices, she had become a full-time student in college. And although the forms were signed and dated before the date of the collision, the medical insurance office refused to accept the forms as they hadn't been received until after the collision had occurred. Therefore, I went the rounds with State Offices for several weeks, trying to obtain alternate medical coverage for my eldest daughter and having to explain she had been in a vehicle collision, was incoherent, and quite literally no longer residing at home by the time I filed for Medicaid on her behalf. She was indeed hospitalized during that time, in San Diego County, California, although my residence was located in Riverside County, California. Contending with insensitive social workers who were ignorant of the fact that while I spoke, my eldest daughter was fighting for her life in a hospital bed. Such telephone discussions were frustrating as well as perplexing during an already stressful situation.

In fact, they were almost as perplexing as my step-mother and former fiancée's mother showing up on the scene, after having decided to spontaneously travel out to the state of California to visit. As we sat conversing in a hospital hallway, outside of Ashley's room, I sat across from each of them while wearing my long wool black trench coat over my clothing. The weather was colder outside. As I sat there, in the corridor, studying each of their countenances, I couldn't help but ponder why the two of them had actually visited and why my biological father hadn't tagged along. Were they there to pray? Or were they there to maliciously savor the most upsetting time of my life? Were they there to start a conflict with the hospital faculty? Were they there to make peace? Were they there hopeful my marriage would end, so I could reconcile with an ex-fiancée? What was the purpose of their visit? Why were they there?!!! I did not know. The only thing my ex-fiancée's mother said was, "This is sad. This is very sad." I respectfully concurred. Meanwhile, in that particular moment, I was sure there were definitely at least two upset couples, me being part of one of the couples. While my spouse and I had our own personal set of marital problems at the time, I still silently considered his feelings. He didn't have to communicate his thoughts out loud, pertaining to his opinion over the two guests from the East Coast. Fortunately, he was at home tending to my two other children. Jason was always instrumental, in the sense of allowing me to confront a potential conflict, alone, while excusing himself from the conversation entirely to go and hide. Nonetheless, I was mindful to be polite and civil to each of the East Coast visitors, while silently praying there wasn't going to be another confrontation, especially once my stepmother started making disdainful remarks about not being "impressed" with the hospital staff overseeing my daughter's medical attention. I didn't agree with her. I was glad Ashley was still alive. Their visit lasted approximately two days. Needless to say, I would've much rather been sitting there talking with my biological dad.

One cool autumn morning, I returned to the gas station that I had mentioned earlier. I walked in unshowered, wearing a yoga outfit, with not an ounce of makeup on. I was over-exhausted and stressed out, yet planning to head to the hospital looking that way anyway...like a "beautiful, hawt mess." Quite honestly, I didn't care what I looked like that day. In fact, I probably hadn't even brushed my hair let alone looked in the mirror before leaving the house, I had tunnel vision, focused on getting two of my children off to school and meeting up with the other at the hospital, with about an hour and a half commute ahead of me.

So anyway, I walked into the gas station and stood at the coffee dispensers mixing my cup of coffee to my preferred Ph, completely oblivious to the gas station attendant and the small crowd of folks standing in a group at the register. That is about the moment the gas station attendant grabbed the microphone next to his register and announced over the store intercom, "Ladies and gentlemen, Wonder Woman has entered the building." Talk about being put in the spotlight while appearing in a state of disarray! I stopped in my tracks for a moment, contemplating my next move. Then I slowly turned around, with my cup of coffee in hand. I looked at the gas station clerk wearing a grin from ear to ear. While the small crowd of customers started to applaud, I'm sure I was blushing, although I was somewhat amused, smiling politely back at my small audience, humbly responding, "Thank you." I didn't feel like a superhero. I didn't think of myself *as* a superhero. I *didn't* look at myself as a superhero. However, the nickname that particular gas station attendant gave me as a result of being amazed by my actions, back on October 12, 2004, stuck with me for several years nonetheless.

That same gas station, along with several other local businesses, collected monetary donations within "Love

Jars". Each "Love Jar" was strategically positioned by my older sister at each store counter along with a brief summary pertaining to Ashley's story and with the intent to promote some form of financial assistance for our family. Unfortunately, in spite of such noble efforts, one "Love Jar" was stolen by an unknown party, containing an estimated $500 inside. The gas station employees were so upset as a result of that theft, to the extent that the incident quite literally reduced a few of their employees to tears. I consoled them while they voiced their complete dismay over the gall (the lack of manners) some individuals have.

On a different occasion, I stopped to hang a flyer that told Ashley's story on a public bulletin board at a Christian gift and book store in San Diego that I had frequented for several years. The manager of the store (a Christian brother) and I spoke for some time about Ashley before bowing our heads to pray. Before I left the store that day, he gave me a bracelet from his wrist to place on Ashley's, which read, "Stay Strong." She wore that bracelet every day for the remaining part of her hospitalization.

"Both death and life are in the power of the tongue..."
—Proverbs 18:21

Thanksgiving Day

On Thanksgiving Day, I received grim news from a neurologist pertaining to Ashley's prognosis. She still lay silent in critical condition, completely comatose. Everyone was hopeful Ashley would pull out of being in a coma. However, she wasn't yet showing any type of response. The neurologist spoke with me, briefly advising we should remain "cautiously optimistic." He suggested Ashley probably would never awaken from the coma. His news was heart-wrenching, to say the least. I wrestled with trying to hold on to hope and trying not to envision my eighteen-year-old daughter spending the rest of her life comatose, in a hospital bed, unresponsive, with absolutely no awareness outside of her being, neither an awareness of others. Needless to say, I respectfully retorted to the neurologist's probable theory pertaining to my daughter's life and assertively said, "In the future, I'd prefer *all* medical discussions pertaining to Ashley be held outside of her hospital room." The doctor and I clearly did *not* concur with one another with regard to Ashley's future prognosis. One of Ashley's friends who happened to be present in the hospital room, interrupted the polite arguing match between the doctor and myself, indicating Ashley was *reacting* to the conversation.

He and I abruptly stopped our disagreement and looked over at Ashley. In that moment, we were silenced, while both the specialist and I simultaneously witnessed Ashley moving one of her knees as to convey, "Hey, I can hear both of you. Stop arguing. I'm *not* a lifeless being. I'm going to pull through this." I rushed to my daughter's side with tears of joy in my eyes, while the neurologist opted to leave the room immediately. I'm guessing he left so abruptly to make a note in Ashley's medical chart and to escape my previous outward distress. I spoke to Ashley in that moment, to see if she would open her eyes, while saying, "Ash! Mommy's here." Ashley's friend also started to talk with her. Witnessing Ashley abruptly moving a single lower extremity on Thanksgiving Day was certainly something worthy of giving thanks for and a praise report worth announcing to my entire family as we all sat down to have Thanksgiving dinner together later that day. That single action from Ashley was the first any of us had seen a hint that she just might wake up, after all. Praise be to God.

During the Thanksgiving season, Ashley's friend visiting from out of state, Ariel, and I ventured to the movie rental store. There we found the character cardboard cutout that Ashley had spoken of before her car accident. Together we decided to carry out the prank

Ashley had planned for her aunt before her collision. We purchased the cardboard cutout, placed a festive hat on it, then strategically set it up in front of my sister's front door, snickering all the while. We rang the doorbell, then ran and hid in the shrubs surrounding the property, waiting patiently for my sister to answer the door. Needless to say, upon opening the door, my sister screamed, as a result of being startled. She said she and her pet beagle about went into "cardiovascular distress on the spot!" Which was an over-exaggeration. However, she was startled, and her dog was indeed barking. Our intent wasn't to frighten them. Meanwhile, Ashley's friend, Ariel, and I were laughing hysterically to the point of tears from our hiding places. My sister's initial reaction was absolutely unexpected, yet priceless. Then we emerged from our hiding places. My sister then laughed as I explained to her that her eldest niece had planned that prank. As I sit here typing about this event, I have no idea what my sister ended up doing with the life-sized character cardboard cutout. However, I still think pulling off that prank on behalf of Ashley, as well as my sister's reaction, was comically amusing.

As the weeks passed, the doctors started to gradually wean Ashley off the pain medications, although she was still very much comatose. Her dad and I watched, nervously and in horror, while the muscles of her lower extremities contracted in atrophy, her arms turning outward in a manner that they weren't created to turn. She no longer looked calm and peaceful while she was sleeping. Her countenance conveyed she was feeling real and almost unbearable physical pain. Her nostrils would flare, while her teeth clenched down. Her vitals were still dangerously high. Her small frame appeared to be sort of convulsing, jerking uncontrollably, while appearing to be struggling to wake up. It was difficult to watch Ashley in that struggle, while the health care team attempted to keep her comfortable and stable. During that time, her dad and I spoke words to attempt to calm her.

During those months, Ashley's dad visited from out of state on a routine basis, sharing intermittent shifts at Ashley's side in the hospital. We also shared a room with two beds at a neighboring temporary housing facility close to the hospital. Seldom were Kevin and I ever in the hospital room together. However, within that temporary housing facility, we could prepare meals and get rest while being in close range of the hospital. One evening, I prepared dinner for him, Ariel, and my-self—occasionally Ariel or one of Ashley's friends would stay there with me. However, during Kevin's visits, he'd make disdainful remarks about the God that I believe in and also question my decisions pertaining to keeping Ashley alive. That being said, there were times when I asked him to leave. On other occasions, he chose to leave, unannounced, on his own accord to avoid another dispute. We were both conflicted over our daughter. Yet we each had a difference of opinion with regard to whether or not we should unplug the life support equipment that was keeping our daughter alive. I wanted to hold on to the promise from my angelic messenger that Ashley would truly miraculously survive, but Kevin was negative and didn't see a miracle about to unfold. However, he made a comment during one conversation about the boldness in the tone of my voice assuring him that Ashley truly would survive. He nervously disclosed, "It was as though someone gave Wendy all the answers." That "someone" was in reference to my close encounter with an angel from God that I had spoken of, after sitting down in the squad car, the morning of October 12th, 2004.

Meanwhile, things weren't okay on the home front. I'd no sooner leave the hospital to check in on my family, than I would return home to a nagging husband. Jason relentlessly lectured me about "spending too much time at the hospital." My two younger children greeted me with hugs, overjoyed to see me, eager to learn how their older sister was doing. They too were praying for a miracle and looked forward to the day when Ashley would be discharged from the hospital to return home with me.

At the time, Jacob was a student attending Christian preschool, being taught and watched over by several educated Christian mentors. His circle of friends and their families were all Christian believers. He enjoyed attending school. Reciting memory verses, prayer, and singing and dancing to praise and worship music were big parts of his day. He hadn't yet had the opportunity to see his eldest sister in the hospital, although some of his adult mentors (members of the clergy) at the church school had. The Christian school and the church that was affiliated with the school had been praying for Ashley as well as for our family. Jacob was aware that his eldest sister was hospitalized and that I wasn't home as often. He hadn't even seen the hospital photographs, other than maybe from the local newspaper of the scene of the collision. Nonetheless, Jacob was resilient and kept an optimistic personality.

However, early on, Ariel wasn't coping as well, and it became even more evident through her grades. Before her sister's collision, Ariel was a high honor roll student, with a grade point average higher than 4.0. Shortly after Ashley's vehicle collision, I received notification from the school. The teachers were concerned because they had seen a sudden drop in Ariel's GPA. That single telephonic conversation would be that one important telephone call advising me that Ariel was also silently grieving, despite the efforts of her church youth group friends. This caused me to rearrange my schedule, after reevaluating how much time I spent at the hospital and at home with my family. I reached out to Ariel and kept her a little bit closer to my side. Fortunately, after I made changes within my schedule, Ariel's GPA went back up. Within a matter of weeks, she was back on course. More than anything, at the time, I think Ariel was scared she'd lose her older sister. I think she felt helpless over the situation. I think she missed my presence at home, as she wasn't accustomed to me not being around on a consistent basis. I was fortunate that she would notify me on my wireless device, asking what time I'd be home or to tattle on her little brother.

Day after day, at the hospital I massaged Ashley's limbs and tended to her basic grooming. I'd sing as well as read scriptures and other inspirational books to her. Sometimes I'd read emails to her from the numerous amounts of individuals who visited and left a message on her website, many of whom I didn't know. Ashley had become a little star, a celebrity, while lying in a coma, completely unaware. Her story captivated many individuals around the globe, but especially in the township we had resided in. Her popularity was astonishing, and it was exciting to visit her website and watch the number of visitors climb. At her bedside sat a portable stereo where I usually left a praise and worship music CD playing at a low decibel. Suddenly the day came when Ashley finally squeezed my hand. Each milestone with regard to Ashley's progress brought tears of joy.

At night, sometimes I'd have dreams of Ashley unscathed. She would be smiling, while having a conversation with me, saying, "Don't worry. I'm going to be fine." In other dreams, she would be sitting up in her hospital bed talking or walking as though she had been restored. Sometimes I would meet up with her in a garden, where there were many banquet tables covered in white linen tablecloths, adorned in beautiful place settings, floral arrangements, as well as flower petals. My two other children were seated at the table with me, while Ashley would be standing, opening a door from a building structure as though anxiously awaiting to greet the next guest. No other people were around. I had no idea how large of a party Ashley planned on hosting. I remember sitting at the table, wondering who was going to walk through the door next. Those dreams often relieved my emotional anguish, allowing me to escape the grim reality for a few moments. But then I would awaken to the REALITY of despair, associated with Ashley's state at that time.

One acquaintance suggested, "Perhaps that dream is what we have to look forward to," making reference to our upcoming reunion in heaven, suggesting that I had experienced a "prophetic dream."

Christmastime

As the Christmas season approached, the skilled health care team was successful in keeping Ashley alive. She showed remarkable progress and eventually graduated from the trauma ward. She was moved to a different floor of the hospital for her continued recovery, as she proceeded to slowly emerge from the coma. Family members and friends were thankful that she was showing good signs of progress. However, we still didn't know how long she'd be hospitalized.

Routinely, Ashley's equipment alarms advised the health care team that she was experiencing respiratory distress as a result of the "plug" (mucus or blood clot) within her lung capacity. The designated respiratory care team and providers would quickly address the situation, in order to ensure Ashley kept breathing. Those moments were scary. They proved that while Ashley was clinically stable, she was still very fragile and had quite a ways to go with regard to her recovery before everyone could relax. God taught me the lesson of practicing true patience during that time.

Late one afternoon, my husband, son, and I visited a retail store in San Diego, California. My son and Jason went in one direction to do some shopping, while I ventured in the other direction also to do some shopping, as Ariel and I had decided to decorate Ashley's hospital room with Christmas décor and make it appear more festive during the month of December.

Life seemed surreal. I was still very much sleep-deprived and stressed out as I browsed the seasonal section within the store. I stood in the aisle staring at the decorations, feeling distraught with grief, in spite of the fact Ashley was making good but slow strides.

Other shoppers busily tended to their shopping while store employees tended to their employment duties. Meanwhile, I stood in a particular aisle, alone, pondering the Christmas decorations for Ashley's hospital room. Then a single song played over the store sound system that caught my attention. It was a song that I had heard countless times, yet this time...the song reduced me to my knees and had me quite literally sobbing and heaving in hysterics. Essentially, a few moments later, that is precisely how my husband and three-year-old son found me in the store...an emotional wreck, on my knees, on the floor of a retail store. I had suppressed my emotions. Trying to remain "strong" for everyone was becoming more complicated. And there, in that retail store, I became undone in a single moment. The upsetting events of the two previous months had finally caught up with me.

Concerned, Jason rushed over to me, pulled me up from the floor, embraced me in his arms while I proceeded to weep over Ashley, both of us wearing our Ashley awareness clothing. The song was none other than the classic Christmas tune, "I'll Be Home for Christmas." I eventually regained my composure, and we proceeded to the store checkout area.

After we left the store that night, we headed to the hospital. Ariel was also wearing an Ashley awareness T-shirt, and she gladly assisted me with decorating her sister's hospital room with a small desktop-size artificial Christmas tree and clear LED lights. We strung delicate brilliant-colored turquoise and iridescent ornaments from its branches, along with coordinating ribbon. Among the decorations were clear resin miniature angel ornaments, strategically and graciously positioned by both Ariel and me, throughout the tiny branches of the Christmas tree. Ashley's room was also graced with a small resin nativity set placed at the base of the tree, gifted to her from a sister from the church.

An array of Christmas greeting cards from an undocumented amount of souls was also on display within her room.

That evening, the hospital staff allowed us to pose for a family group photograph together, captured with a digital camera. This would be the first time Jacob would be allowed to see his eldest sister since the day of her vehicle collision.

That year, I had that single image transferred onto professional Christmas greeting cards along with the sentiment of "Peace on Earth," and I managed to send the cards out to family, friends, business colleagues, and others during the Christmas season. A copy of THAT particular card went as far as the nation of Africa, to a child that I sponsored for a time and had written to overseas through means of a Christian-funded organization, a child whom my family had never actually met in person. Nonetheless, upon receiving the greeting card and learning of Ashley's condition, that child informed me that he would pray for Ashley's recovery.

Before Christmas Day 2004, Ashley continued to make exceptional progress and was ready to be transported to a sub-acute hospital, also located within southern California, for further recovery and rehabilitation. Ashley had continued to slowly emerge from coma, opening her eyes for a few moments at a time, showing she was somewhat alert. Everyone, including the health care team, was ecstatic. Although her eyes were opening, however, she was still unresponsive, staring off into the distance as though she was millions of miles away. After a few moments, she then would close her eyes as though going back to a state of peaceful rest. I had the responsibility of removing and transporting all of her personal belongings from the hospital, over to the next hospital room, waiting for her at the hospital she would be transferred to, all in an attempt to assist with getting her settled in. Meanwhile, she was transported by an ambulance. What's more, I was no longer staying in the housing facility next door to the hospital; instead I was back at home every single night.

Upon my arrival, I noted the sub-acute hospital was much smaller in comparison to the previous hospital. However, the environment and surrounding area was very cheery and well maintained. They didn't have as many individuals frequenting their facility.

During Christmas Eve that year, I spent a conservative amount of time speaking with Ashley, while tending to the details within her assigned hospital room, mindful to also include the soft, soothing sound of Christmas music at her bedside before leaving the hospital to join family for our regular Christmas traditions. Nestled at the base of Ashley's hospital room

Christmas tree was an array of both Christmas as well as birthday gifts for her. Around the world, countless individuals and families would be celebrating Christmas, while Ashley would be turning nineteen years of age the following day, completely unaware. She was in a semi-coma at a Level 1, according to the Coma Scale. With regard to the Coma Scale, there are eight levels: Level 0 being completely incoherent and Level 8 being most optimal, as well as completely alert.

On Christmas Day, Ashley was visited by several family members as we congregated in her shared hospital room. There was no birthday cake or ice cream served, as Ashley still couldn't eat any foods orally and was receiving only stomach tube feedings. However, we were blessed that Ashley opened her eyes several times, as I carefully opened each of her gifts for her, advising her whom each of the gifts were from. Among the gifts were two separate posters of two characters from the last film she had seen and commented on frequently, before her vehicle collision...a popular pirate film. One poster was that of her favorite character, the other poster was that of his ally in the film. Both posters were gifted from two different relatives. We wasted no time hanging the posters on the wall of Ashley's hospital room, directly in view where she could stare at them. I suppose my sister and I both secretly figured, apart from one another, that Ashley should have something nice to stare at while being a patient in a hospital. No matter how obnoxious it may have seemed at the time, not one health care provider stopped us from transforming Ashley's hospital room to soon take on the appearance of that of a usual nineteen-year-old female's bedroom. For that I'm very thankful. Several hospital employees also commented how they enjoyed sitting in Ashley's room.

A New Year's Eve Candlelight Vigil

"Candles to Light the Night for Crash Victim" was the newspaper title. Specifically, pink candles were illuminated across the United States in a candle vigil scheduled on New Year's Eve on behalf of Ashley. A citizen in Australia had also participated in the candle vigil. The color pink was chosen, as that is Ashley's favorite color. Most of those who had gathered at my sister's residence lit their candles as scheduled. Both Ariel and Jacob participated in the candle lighting event on behalf of their older sister. Jacob required assistance, due to the fact that he was still a toddler at the time. He was so cute and thoughtful, although he was oftentimes not allowed to visit with Ashley during the earliest days of her hospitalization. Other individuals also gathered at my sister's residence. After the vigil started, I left in route for the hospital, alone.

Once I arrived, I noted the hospital staff was conducting a small New Year's Eve party in their break room as I made my way past the nurses' desk and proceeded in the direction of my daughter's hospital room. As I walked into the room, I turned Ashley's radio off and grabbed the remote to her television set. Then I sat down and found the station broadcasting the New Year's celebration at Times Square, in New York City. I sat there fidgeting, talking with Ashley, advising her that it was New Year's Eve and that I was there to ring the New Year in with her. Ashley opened her eyes for a few moments, unresponsive, as though listening, or rather to simply acknowledge my presence. Yet, she still stared off into the distance, what seemed a million miles away. After a few minutes, she'd close her eyes once again. Close to midnight, one of the nurses found me sitting in the corner alone next to Ashley, and she brought me a plate of food from their break room. I thanked the nurse for being so thoughtful. The other patient who shared the same room with Ashley was an elderly woman. She started speaking with me from the other side of the curtain. She asked if I could turn her television on for her as she wanted to watch the New Year's celebration also. So, I assisted her. We shared polite conversation for a few moments before I returned to Ashley's side. At the point when the ball dropped in New York City, both Ashley and the other patient were sound asleep. Therefore, I kissed Ashley's forehead and whispered in her ear, "Happy New Year." Then I turned each television set off, dimmed the lights, and left the hospital en route for my residence.

I received several photographs via email, via the website, as well as via USPS of those who had lovingly participated in Ashley's candlelight vigil, posing with their pink candles and posting well wishes and/or prayers for Ashley's continued progress. Some of those photographs were added to the website, while other snapshots were placed into a scrapbook that I put together for Ashley. It was memoir made exclusively for her, accurately archiving the course of this particular storm within in her life, along with guestbook pages as a personal keepsake.

At the turn of the New Year and the months that followed, God bestowed many blessings and answered countless prayers with regard to Ashley's recovery. She continued to slowly climb up the numbers in the Coma Scale and progressed. Still, though, the health care providers cautioned, "In the event that Ashley completely emerges from coma, she may have symptoms of amnesia as a result of the traumatic brain injury that she sustained at the time of her vehicle collision. She might experience no recollection of who she is or who her relatives and friends are. She might have no recollection of her vehicle collision at all. Yet, it is very possible that her memory could still be intact." This news was perplexing for me as Ashley's mother as I braced myself for the unknown. Fortunately, over the course of her life I had kept a school memory book, a collection of photographs, as well as a conservative number of family videos that I thought could aid Ashley in recollection, in the event she emerged from the coma with symptoms of amnesia.

Ashley had started moving and lifting her right leg. Yet, her responding to verbal commands was infrequent. We weren't sure where she was cognitively.

I recall an elderly patient confined to a wheelchair who would roll himself down the sub-acute hospital corridor, day after day, in order to find his way to the doorway of Ashley's hospital room. Before Ashley's admittance at that hospital, he wasn't acquainted with our family. However, upon learning of Ashley's story, each day he would sit outside of her room, speaking with her and waiting for her to open her eyes. The elderly man was concerned and perplexed over Ashley's condition and upset over the fact she was in such a battle at such a young age. Therefore, he'd try to get Ashley's attention and ask for her to look at him, while sitting in the doorway just off to the right of the foot of her bed. During those days Ashley would continue to stare straight ahead as though focused intensely on something in the distance. Her eyes weren't tracking up, down, or side to side, only straight ahead. Her countenance was completely expressionless. Yet, day after day, like family and friends, that kind elderly man refused to give up on her, along with the health care team addressing her medical attention.

That thoughtful individual claimed to also be "Praying for a healing miracle for Ashley." Then one wonderful day, it finally happened for him. God answered his prayer, while he sat in the entryway of Ashley's hospital room speaking with her. He finally was successful at getting Ashley's attention. She opened her eyes, slowly tracked (looked over) in his direction, and stared directly back at him. The elderly man cried tears of joy. Once I arrived out at the hospital that afternoon, he wasted no time to tell me his praise report. He was the first to obtain a visual response from Ashley and the first to make contact beyond the barrier in her brain that seemingly held her as a captive, as though she were in an entranced state. Upon receiving the news of Ashley accomplishing yet another milestone in her recovery, countless souls rejoiced. Within a few days, Ashley's eyes started tracking, more frequently, showing incredible progress. However, her optical range (her eyesight) was significantly compromised. The left eye pupil was affixed, open, nonresponsive to light or dark. The right eye pupil was functioning as it should. Ashley was later diagnosed with what is referred to as diplopia. Her left eye pupil and eye range never improved to what it was before her vehicle collision, unfortunately. However, she still had the ability of sight.

However, by the end of the month of January 2005, she was squeezing hands with her right hand upon prompting and responding "yes" to simplistic questions, by means of closing her eyelids, learning an alternative way to communicate. She had a tracheostomy still in place, and tubes had surgically been placed in her larynx area three months previous, preventing her from speaking. Yet, they provided oxygen to her being, nonetheless.

She was rolling her right shoulder area, slowly responding to and following simple commands. She started moving the fingers on her right hand, experiencing moments of trying to reach for, grasp, and hold objects set in front of her, on her bedtable. Ashley gradually pulled out of the coma and started moving her lower-right-side extremities (arm/leg). One afternoon it seemed as if she had taken a giant leap in her recovery, suddenly gaining use of her right hand, pulling at the linens covering her. She intermittently would shake her fist in a violent, erratic sort of manner. At that point, she was deemed at about a Level 4 on the Coma Scale, while experiencing a certain level of discomfort. Therefore, I stood back while her team of health care team addressed her medical needs.

Ashley was moved to a new hospital room, working every day on her eye and hand coordination, with both her physical and her occupational therapists. We noted one Friday afternoon that she was erratically moving her fingers and violently resumed shaking her fist, in a sort of pattern. The medical team explained this behavior (anger) as "normal" for an individual waking from a coma, especially for those who have experienced "traumatic brain injury."

That evening, after I had left the hospital and joined my family, I made mention of this during dinner conversation. Ariel advised she wanted to visit with her sister as she was off from school. Therefore, the following day, both Ariel and I arrived together out at the sub-acute hospital. We entered the room, and a nurse who was tending to Ashley commented she was "still shaking her fist." I sat down next to Ashley and held her hand in mine for a few moments, trying to console her. Suddenly, Ashley withdrew her hand from mine. I stared at Ashley, wondering what was going on in that beautiful mind of hers. Meanwhile, my other daughter, Ariel, was standing in the doorway of the room and let out a gasp. Through broken sobs, Ariel inquired, "Mom, how long has Ashley been doing that?!!!" I glanced over at Ariel, who had tears in her eyes, and responded, "A few days now." That's when Ariel informed both the nurse and me that Ashley was trying to communicate using basic one-handed sign language, a language that both my daughters had learned from the time they were small children. They each had been acquainted with individuals who are deaf, but sign language was a form of communication that I obviously never had learned. Ariel drew closer to observe her older sister intently. She advised us that Ashley was repetitiously signing the letter T. I remember leaving the room immediately and running down the hospital corridor to the nurse's desk to inform them, "Ashley's making a fair attempt to communicate with us through means of sign language. Please inform her speech therapist!"

During the weeks that followed, Ashley continued to use hand gestures and one-handed sign language to communicate, although she would tire out very easily. Her aunt and I assisted the medical team with working on Ashley's eye and hand coordination. We handed her a Magna-Doodle to write messages on. On one occasion, as Ashley continued to emerge from the coma, I tested her memory out. I handed her the Magna-Doodle board and stylus, then proceeded to ask her this question: "Ashley, do you know who I am?"

I waited patiently for her response, as at the time, her responses were delayed. Ashley looked me straight in the eye, both of us studying each other's countenance. She then looked at the Magna-Doodle, picked up the stylus, and wrote these words, "You have no idea who you are." She then rested the writing instrument down and stared back at me with a very serious-looking expression on her face. I laughed so hard, I cried. Ashley smirked. In that single wonderful moment, I knew my daughter's sense of humor and intuitive nature was still intact. Other times, it was as though she was studying my expression, maybe my reaction, searching for answers.

So, I said, while chuckling, "Okay... Allow me to rephrase the question." Then I gently handed the Magna-Doodle back to her. I then said, "I...know who I,..am. However, I...want to know if *you* know who I am. Ashley, who am I to you?" Ashley stared at me for a few moments, then looked at the Magna-Doodle board. Then she proceeded to pick up the stylus once again and wrote, "Mom." I cried tears of joy, as within that moment, I had confirmation that my daughter had recollection of who I was.

During the weeks that followed, Ashley continued to work on her eye/hand coordination, making a fair attempt to regain her fine motor skills, while relearning how to write. Her penmanship was scribbly and difficult to read at times. Once she started communicating through means of both basic sign language as well as writing on a note tablet, though, we took turns asking one another questions pertaining to various subjects. This is how I learned she had short-term memory loss, a guesstimated one years' worth of memory loss before she was in the collision. She'd ask questions such as, "Where am I?"; "What state are we in?"; "What hospital am I in?"; "How long have I been in the hospital?"; "What happened to me?"; "Where's my boyfriend?"; and "How old am I?" I would sit at her bedside and patiently answer each of her questions accurately, while studying her facial expressions. Each day she would ask the same questions over and over again. Then I'd ask her a few questions. She conveyed having no recollection of graduating from high school or starting college. She had no recollection of breaking up with her high school sweetheart. She presumed he might have been in the vehicle collision with her, had gotten seriously injured, reasoning that was why he never visited her during her hospitalization. I assured her that wasn't the case. I explained that she and her high school sweetheart had broken up before graduation. I told her she had been very sad the evening they broke off. However, I also told her that I was there to comfort her that evening. Once I advised Ashley about their breakup, having had no previous recollection of the event, she seemed very saddened. However, I advised her that she had started dating another individual after she'd started college. I advised Ashley she was en route to meet her new boyfriend for breakfast at the time of the collision. Ashley had no recollection of the other fellow whatsoever, neither did he visit her over the course of her hospitalization except for one occasion.

Assisting Ashley during her time of repressed memory was a challenge, and yes, it was sometimes upsetting. I was fortunate to have video-taped her high school graduation. Therefore, one afternoon I brought my camcorder to the hospital. I asked their faculty if there was a television that could be placed in Ashley's hospital room for the day. One of the hospital personnel brought a television over right away. That afternoon, we sat down and watched Ashley's high school graduation ceremony together. In fact, Ashley viewed that film on several occasions, staring curiously at herself. Yet, her countenance was sometimes equivalent to that of a harsh critic. She seemed upset at her former self upon seeing herself on the television screen within a few of the scenes. To date, I do not know what upset her.

I think the most compelling conversation I had with Ashley during that time was the day I informed her of the approximate duration of time she had been in the hospital, comatose and then still considered "semi-comatose." I advised her that she had been asleep for several months. Ashley matter-of-factly responded, while writing on her note tablet, "I've been communing with Jesus and the saints—angels." In that moment, Ashley, without being prompted, had answered the number-one grueling question that had been nagging at my spirit and mind for months, other than the question of whether she would survive. And in that moment, her testimony literally reduced me to tears of joy once again, causing me to kneel at her side. There I was in my daughter's hospital room, sobbing, praising Jesus for confirming through my child that during the times she was comatose, she wasn't lying there in darkness, but rather her spirit was in the presence of a loving Savior, the Physician of all physicians, as well as communing with other heavenly beings. She wrote, "Angels." Hallelujah!

Ashley continued to speak frequently pertaining to her tour of heavenly places on her notepad. Of course,

I had a few questions. Most of my questions Ashley would answer right away, while other times, she'd respond with a sort of subtle authority, writing, "You're not supposed to ask that," causing me to laugh out loud. I then would hug her and thank her. Without a doubt, she had an unmistakable awareness of the things she could disclose and the things she couldn't. I respected that and moved on with either a different discussion or a question.

There was a point when my husband at the time had left town to visit his relatives out in the Midwest. They asked how Ashley was progressing. He was at a loss for words, incapable of answering their many inquiries. One of my very brazen in-laws, at the time, was so bold to reprimand him in front of the other family members during the gathering, saying, "You still sleep and live with your wife in the same house... *Right?!!!* Then how is it you have no idea how your stepdaughter is doing in the hospital?!!!" He wasn't sure how to respond as a result of being caught in his own negligence. Therefore, I referred his relatives to the website in the event they wanted to keep up to date with regard to Ashley, in order to also allow them an opportunity to sign her internet guestbook at their leisure.

Resurrection Sunday

Resurrection Sunday, also known as Easter, is a Christian festival celebrating the day of Jesus Christ's resurrection. My husband, my two youngest children, and I headed to the hospital to meet with Ashley and to attend the hospital church service together as a family. This was the first time my family had had the opportunity to attend church service together in quite a few months. After the service, we participated in the festivities hosted outside of the hospital in the courtyard. I was so glad to have the opportunity to take Ashley outdoors for a stroll throughout the hospital courtyard, instead of her being confined indoors, as the weather had permitted.

W.L. Adams & Ashley, outside of a Subacute hospital in San Diego County, CA, in the Spring of 2005.

7

Make Some Noise

"Make a joyful noise unto God..."
—Psalm 66:1

During the spring months of 2005, Ashley's health continued to improve, and she was finally capable of breathing on her own again, with the need of a respirator machine. Therefore, the respiratory tracheostomy tubes were extracted from her airway. The first word she spoke was a very breathy whisper sounding like "Mom."

Ashley had spent approximately four months at the sub-acute hospital and had made most of her progress there, before finally being discharged and transported to a different hospital for further recovery and to receive rehabilitation services. Once again, I had the liberty of packing her belongings up and transporting everything to a third hospital located in San Diego, California. Before I left the sub-acute facility that day, the staff members employed there learned that I was compiling a scrapbook for Ashley, as I had taken pictures of some of their staff members with my camera. They also had the opportunity to sign Ashley's guestbook. A few of the staff members advised they loved Ashley and advised that they'd miss her very much. They were very good to my daughter while she was in their care, treating her with the utmost respect and dignity. Before I left, they made a simple, humble request, asking that their photographs be shaped into that of "hearts." I upheld to their request while I was putting the scrapbook together several years later.

Once I arrived at the rehabilitation hospital, the first thing I noted was that it was gloomy in comparison to the previous hospitals. For instance, the light fixture over Ashley's hospital bed appeared to be broken and looked as though it was about to fall off the wall. The paint on the walls was a color that made the room feel *dreary* and depressing. Ashley had been assigned to a room located all the way at the end of the hallway, not within close range of the nurses' desk. I sat there in Ashley's hospital room, waiting for the new medical team to arrive with their forms that required my signature, while silently observing the hospital that desperately needed new renovations and coordinating new curtains—perhaps even the intervention of an electrician. I made a fair attempt to make Ashley's new hospital room appear more welcoming, first addressing the light fixture dangling on the wall. At the time, my spouse was an entrepreneur, a general contractor in the industry of painting properties. I informed Jason after returning home that evening, "You might want to consult with the rehabilitation hospital and leave a few of your business cards in their main office. That place could really use a new paint job, with brighter colors. Essentially, the inside of the rehabilitation hospital rooms remind me of a military barracks. Everything within the rooms seemed out-of-date." He, being the United States Marine Corps veteran that he is, I thought would understand. I perceived in the event he submitted a bid and was hired for the job, he could be closer to both Ashley and me during the daytime. Perhaps we could even commute together. I don't know if he ever delivered a business card to their hospital office.

However, shortly after Ashley was settled into the rehabilitation hospital, I learned that one of the employees there was a member of the former Christian church that I had attended. I recognized her at once and was happy to see a familiar face. It gave me great comfort to know she was there. Her office was located just down the hallway from Ashley's hospital room. Several members from their church committee and choir regularly visited Ashley during her hospitalization.

A church brother, Felipe, a dear friend of mine since my teenage years, notified me telephonically, advising he had visited the hospital on a few occasions, only to learn that Ashley had been moved before his last visit. He asked what hospital she was transported to. Therefore, I informed him.

Ashley resumed physical, occupational, and speech therapy during this last leg of her hospitalization. During her stay, we soon discovered other patients there, both male and female, within her same age category. They also were wounded victims of catastrophic vehicle collisions. We met with and spoke with some of their families. There were two patients other than Ashley who were very verbally hostile as a result of their traumatic head injuries, yelling out all hours of the day. This especially would upset Ashley. On one occasion, while my daughter was seated in front of the nurses' desk in a wheelchair, next to another patient seated in a wheelchair who was hollering vulgarities at the top of her lungs, Ashley managed to roll her wheelchair in the direction of the other patient and was winding up for a one-handed physical altercation with the other patient. Fortunately, the nurses quickly intervened, sort of playing referee between Ashley and the other patient. After that day, they decided to keep the two of them apart. However, the young man across the hallway from Ashley's hospital room was certainly just as brash. It was explained to me by the neurologists that this behavior is normal during the healing process for those who have been in comas and/or sustained severe traumatic brain injury, that is patients hollering and being relatively aggressive. However, nonetheless, I think the other patients hollering was simply upsetting to my daughter. There wasn't a whole lot that I could do, other than close the door to Ashley's room, to subdue the sound.

Ashley continued to communicate on her notepad, countless times, stating that she wanted to have the ability to speak fluently again. She would practice various exercises with the speech pathologist. Most of Ashley's communication was done in writing. However, she eventually progressed to the extent that she could say in a whispery sounding tone, "Mom," "Ariel," and "I...love...you..." She experienced difficulty with enunciating most phonics. Yet, she gained the ability back to partially raise her arms and affectionately hug those who visited her with sincere gratitude. She was grateful to be alive.

Then came the day when Ashley was given an electronic communication board, preprogrammed with simplistic commands, to advise the staff if she was hungry or thirsty or if her body temperature was comfortable. She enjoyed pressing the key for, "I'm hot," while

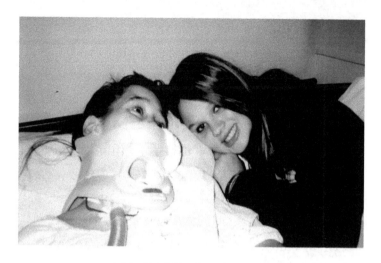

Ashley & Ariel in the spring, 2005.

giggling in a mischievous manner and putting a spin on the context, causing those within listening range to laugh along with her. She wasn't making a reference to her body temperature but rather to that of her appearance, while confirming her wittiness as well as sense of humor.

My cousin and her daughter frequently visited, bringing Ashley fresh floral arrangements from my cousin's floral shop on a regular basis. Therefore, Ashley always had a fresh bouquet of fragrant fresh flowers on the table within her room, which we appreciated.

Eventually, Ashley progressed to being able to eat foods naturally again, as the hospital staff slowly weaned Ashley from stomach tube feedings. The staff started Ashley on nectar consistency foods and fluids. They allowed me to feed her applesauce. I was so nervous the first few times I fed her—but my cousin never was. Once she learned Ashley was capable of eating food, she decided to cook and fearlessly smuggle into the hospital Ashley's *favorite* meal, a Pacific Islander specialty: chicken adobo and white rice. My cousin proceeded to feed the meal to Ashley as I sat there supervising, concerned the entire time over the hospital staff's reaction in the event we all got caught. I sort of sat there adorning a sheepish grin, accompanied with some nervous laughter, the moment we ended up getting caught. The staff member's reaction was different from what I had expected. She was glad to learn Ashley was tolerating foods of a greater consistency. We promised that bringing in food from outside of the hospital wasn't going to be a habitual occurrence. Eventually, Ashley's stomach feeding tube was removed as she graduated to being able to eat solid foods, at either a pureed and/or a minced consistency. The therapists were very successful at reteaching Ashley how to feed herself, with the one hand she had regained the use of.

On occasion, her younger brother, Jacob, my little California boy, four years old at the time, would accompany me to the hospital for a short visit. Sometimes he would sit on the other bed in her hospital room. Other times, he would sit on one of the hospital chairs, conversing, watching the television as well as sometimes playing quietly with his toy cars and such, while I'd tend to Ashley. He enjoyed visiting the hospital and seeing that his eldest sister was recovering. His presence there was like sunlight to the room. He was always a happy child, with the light of the glory of God illuminating his countenance. He was very glad the moment his sister could eat snacks again. They both liked applesauce and fruit juice. They both enjoyed watching animated films together over a portable screen/DVD player.

As Ashley's family and friends learned she was alert and interacting during the daytime hours, I installed an answering machine to her hospital room telephone. They understood, after the tracheostomy tubing was removed, it was soon discovered Ashley was incapable of speaking as she used to, in her regular-sounding voice. Although she could say some words, her tone of voice was closer to that of a whisper. She was deemed "aphonic," otherwise known as mute. Yet, we remained hopeful she would gain back the ability to speak. However, she did have the ability to hear. Therefore, installing the answering machine enabled family and friends to notify Ashley, telephonically. She could listen to their voice over the speaker as they left a message. One of her former male colleagues, Jody, would call her telephone extension and recite scripture messages to her, causing Ashley to smile. Other messages he left were very comical, causing the entire staff and Ashley to laugh out loud. He once proposed marriage to her over the answering machine, when he prepared to enlist in the Armed Forces. Another male friend, Henry, also from the Midwest, pleaded with her via email to marry him, instead of like the other guy who was leaving messages over her answering machine. Those two male friends bantering over Ashley's hand in marriage made us laugh so hard. Ashley, being most familiar with their sense of humor compared to the rest of us, responded a whispery sounding "No!" to both of them. Yet, she was truly amused by each of them nonetheless.

The convenience in having such an electronic device also enabled me to telephonically inform Ashley as well as the staff as to when I was headed in route to the hospital and also enabled me to say "good night" to her around bedtime while I was at home.

Over time, Ashley was gradually gaining back the use of her right side. Yet she still didn't have much use of her left side. At this point, she was experiencing high tone and wearing arm splints with springs a few hours out of the day. I recall her raising her right hand to her mouth and blowing kisses to convey love and appreciation. On one occasion, I brought her video game system into the hospital and plugged it in to a television monitor, as an effort to encourage her with some form of entertainment, especially the former activities in which she had been proficient. At first, Ashley seemed thrilled to see her video game system. However, once I handed her the game controller device, she was abruptly reminded she had only regained use of one hand. Therefore, in frustration, she threw the piece of electronic equipment across the room like a Frisbee. I hadn't anticipated that reaction. The video game system crashed to the floor. I patiently walked over and picked it up without scolding her. Incidentally, she never attempted to play with that video game system again. However, I searched diligently for a one-handed game controller game system as an alternative. I was empathetic to the fact Ashley was anxious, infuriated, and frustrated as a result of her new inabilities. I wanted to see her reach her goals. Her most desired goal was the ability to walk again, instead of being confined to a wheelchair for the rest of her life.

During those sorts of days, I would embrace her while we both wept. There were countless occasions when I'd patiently explain to Ashley, "Listen, it's the same race. However, your abilities have changed. That means the tools and instruments you must learn to work with are different from before. However, once again, *it is the same race*. It's okay to be angry for a time. But don't allow anger to consume you. I'm still praying for your progress. Trust me. If purchasing the ability for you to walk and talk again was something I could buy off a store shelf, I would purchase those abilities for you at once. That being said, let's focus and rejoice over the things you can still do without someone's assistance." The race I was referring to when I was comforting my child was nothing more than...the race of life. Sometimes I felt as though nothing I could say would comfort her as she panicked over discovering she was crippled, while other times my words were like a soothing balm to her restless heart.

During the spring, Ashley had recovered enough that she could be strolled outside of the hospital in a wheelchair. She enjoyed being outside and oftentimes wanted to stop next to a pink rosebush. There she'd take in the scent of the fragrant rose blooms and pick a single rosebud that she would give to someone else after we had returned to the hospital. Ashley was incredibly selfless and so very fortunate to be alive.

In early June 2005, Ashley was placed in front of a computer, and she was able to type a simple message: "I love mom." It was clear she could still read, spell, and write as a means to communicate. She typed her name under the little note and then printed it out to give to me. I was fortunate my child had survived something so horrific. And I was very thankful she still had the ability to communicate.

As time elapsed, Ashley was adamant about wanting to return "home" instead of being confined within the parameters of a hospital room and its courtyard each day. She would make that request frequently and then retort, "Why?!!!" in a whisper-sounding response once I advised her that her health wasn't strong enough to be released from the hospital's care just yet. She'd argue, *"I am!"* Ashley would start crying once our daily visits were over and it was time for me to leave for home. Leaving her there, day after day, burdened my heart. Subsequently, Ashley's youth pastor also experienced similar conversations with her during his visits. He stated it was everything he could do to not wrap her up in a blanket and carry her home to me.

I'll note that God invented our tears. Tears are a normal reaction to a heartbreaking situation. However, tears are also a form of emotional healing. There were times when I'd visit the hospital, crawl right into Ashley's hospital bed, and sob uncontrollably. Ashley would wipe the tears from my face, silently comforting me. On one occasion, two nurses walked in her room and then turned back around. One nurse respectively advised the other, "Ashley and her mom need some time alone right now." What the medical team at that hospital didn't know was that while most of us were looking forward to Ashley being discharged, there was a lot of arguing going on at home, specifically between me and my husband. I hope that you never find yourself in a situation where you have to choose between two individuals whom you genuinely love and care about, especially in the middle of a challenging situation equivalent to the one my family was faced with during that time.

I prayed that God would help guide my steps, completely aware that most healthy couples' marriages don't last beyond two years after such a distressing event. Nonetheless, I remained a faithful wife and a devout mother.

8

Conflicts with Mainstream Media and Marketing

Ashley's story initially was broadcasted by means of the news media as well as her website. Thoughtful business cards created by my sister went out into distribution from coast to coast with the intent to promote awareness of Ashley's story as well as market a fund-raiser that could be accessed through her website; clothing and other items were for sale, with the proceeds going toward Ashley's medical care.

I encountered conflicts with being misquoted during one media interview, as well as by those who created and added updates to the website early on. There was a high level of demands from Ashley's "fan base," especially when her website went without a daily update. In such times, there was nothing new to report pertaining to her prognosis, and I was busy tending to the care of my family.

Other problems with the website were that I started getting stalked by men, one of whom figured out where my residence was located, based off of the information he obtained from the website. Other individuals whom we weren't acquainted with targeted Ashley, visiting the hospital and imposing themselves without permission while I wasn't there. Which infuriated me.

Conclusively, while the website initially was a blessing, it soon turned into a catalyst that brought on a number of disagreements within the family, along with an array of unwanted problems—the sort of fame that ultimately led to our residence being broke into, scaring my children, and causing me to become incredibly hypervigilant. The website was shut down permanently within four years after it was brought into cyber-existence.

Benefit Concert

A benefit concert for Ashley was held at a public school in the township where we resided, after having been promoted over a radio station in southern California. Aspiring talented entertainers put on a program, and over twenty-three small businesses and major corporations contributed to the fund-raiser held on behalf of my daughter.

9

Ashley's Homecoming

"Ashley, you are my favorite superhero..."
—Ariel Adams

The bedroom that I prepared for Ashley's homecoming was located on the first level of my 2,200-square-foot residence. The entryway to her room had double doors. The room itself was painted and decorated with different shades of pink and accented with antique white trim and an armoire, complete with new carpeting. I strategically customized her bedroom closet with white space-saver shelving and cabinets to leave as much open space available within the room. A standard, electronically operated hospital bed was adorned with stylish coordinating linens and window coverings.

The bathroom located next to Ashley's bedroom was demolished, and then restored and renovated with new paint, a coordinating stone tile countertop, new flooring, and a roll-in shower accompanied with a shower chair. Two thirds of the first level of the home was also tiled off in the same color stone tiles for the purpose of an individual confined to a wheelchair being able to maneuver around practically effortlessly.

While we prepared for Ashley's homecoming, there was a 5.6 earthquake in southern California on the morning of June 12, 2005. I was at home that morning and not at the hospital until later in the day. I was fortunate that the earthquake didn't cause any major devastation to our home, nor to the medical facility where Ashley was staying. Nonetheless, I wondered if she was frightened.

One warm summer day in June 2005, Ashley was finally released from the hospital to return home after nine grueling months of hospitalization. That was a joyous day for her, my family, and many of our relatives, friends, and acquaintances.

As Ashley's paternal aunt, cousin, and I turned down the street in route to my residence, neighborhood children and adults were standing alongside the street cheering and applauding. A group of children started running excitedly after my vehicle. They followed us all the way to my driveway, anxiously waiting to see Ashley. She was greeted with an ample number of hugs, while many individuals were reduced to tears of joy.

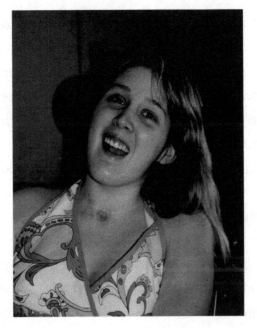

Ashley, after being released from the hospital, 2005.

They were so glad Ashley had survived. Many of them remembered the day of the collision—the roadways being blocked off, the rescue vehicles, and the debris from the two vehicles involved. Many of the families had been following the news, anxiously praying and waiting for Ashley to return home. Ashley was absolutely ecstatic to receive such a warm welcome, although she was still extremely fragile.

That evening I hosted a small quiet "welcome home" celebration dinner, for her with a conservative number of guests, including both relatives and friends. At the time, I was worried about her experiencing too much brain stimulation. The trauma she had sustained to her brain caused her to get upset easily over a variety of factors. She liked her trendy-looking, renovated bedroom, and she enjoyed visiting with friends and family who had come to visit.

My children, my niece, and I had nine months of time to make up for. We were so happy Ashley was home. But reintroducing her back into civilization was going to take some time. However, I believed taking her to the places that she had enjoyed frequenting before her accident and reacquainting her with some of the folks whom she had no recollection of was important, while it also gave her a sense of normalcy.

Meanwhile, amidst a new renovation modification project, Jason decided to make himself scarce, and so he booked travel arrangements for himself to leave town for a few weeks to go visit his relatives. I wasn't sure why he decided to schedule a vacation at such an inopportune time. Certainly, his vacation plans caused a huge argument between us.

At home, I placed a notepad and a dinner bell close to Ashley's side for the purpose of drawing, conversing, and to alert me if she needed something. One of the first things Ashley wrote down after returning home was, "Why is he still here?" In that moment, without prompting, my eldest daughter had just communicated she recalled the conversation she and I had before her vehicle collision took place. I waited until my spouse was out of the house before I responded to Ashley's question. Subsequently, some of her straightforward questions and comments would cause me to laugh.

There were no absolute answers with regard to how much memory she had retained, or where she was on a talent or academic level. Such things were only an educated guess. Independently, I guesstimated she was at about a Level 7 on the Coma Scale. Nonetheless, several times a week, I'd prepare a little mathematical test for her and test her basic math skills. Other times, I tested her artistic skills, a field of study in which she had excelled and in which she had received previous awards. Ashley did very well with basic addition, subtraction, multiplication, and division problems, and for that I was grateful. However, with artistry, she would stare blank-faced at the canvas, resting on a tabletop easel, along with the other art supplies within her reach. Much to my surprise, Ashley was disinterested in drawing, painting, or sculpting.

Knowledgeable of Ashley's former artistic interests and capabilities, I decided to purchase seven wooden crosses from an arts and crafts store for Ashley to paint and decorate, as a means of both occupational as well as recreational therapy and to reawaken her artistic skills. I helped Ashley with this project as her right arm would tire easily. It took approximately two months for her to paint all of the crosses—an average of one cross per week. She personalized each cross and wrote a note to each individual to whom she wished to give a cross, with some assistance from me. Ashley's fine motor skills weren't present, so it was my job to dry the rose buds out, then glue them along with a message of Ashley's choosing on each cross, with a hot glue gun. I also touched up any areas that she had missed with leftover paint. Once the gifts were complete, we wrapped them together, anxiously waiting to distribute the crosses to unsuspecting relatives. While Ashley still had use of her right hand, we never painted one for our residence. I suppose the reason for that is because we weren't thinking about ourselves and our home was already filled with inspirational messages, as well as faith-based artwork and sculptures.

Ashley painting at home, 2006.

One warm summer day, the pastor of our home church, a retired police officer instructor, and other church members finally enjoyed seeing my children and I make an appearance out at church together. He was the sort of pastor who noted if any members from the flock weren't present from one Sunday to the next. Therefore, he was so happy to see Ashley after her being absent for almost a year's time. After the service, I was in a conversation with another church family member. I turned around and caught Ashley as well as Pastor John comparing their biceps with one another, showing each other how *strong* they were. Ashley was silently conveying, "See that, Pastor? I'm strong. I'm very, very, *very* strong. Check out my bicep!" Then we watched the pastor roll up his sleeve and flex for Ashley. They both started laughing, causing their audience to laugh also.

At home, Ashley wrote frequently about communing with God in heaven and with her ancestors who had graduated to heaven. One afternoon, she mentioned visiting with my paternal grandparents in heaven while she was comatose. The interesting thing about this discussion is that before the collision, Ashley had never had the opportunity to meet my beloved grandfather, as he had passed away before she was conceived. Yet she advised me that while they were communing in heaven together, my grandfather had asked her to tell me that he loved me—the very words that I had longed to hear since I was a child after learning of my grandfather passing away. She also advised me that Jesus had allowed my grandmother to accompany her back from the realm of heaven. Our discussion, that day, literally reduced me to my knees and tears once again, there within her bedroom while she sat in her hospital bed. I wasn't prepared for, nor did I expect, these discussions that Ashley shared with me pertaining to her visit to heaven. I truly believe everything she disclosed.

I happened to mention these discussions with her neurologist during one medical appointment. The doctor advised me, "Eighty percent of patients who sustain similar injuries to Ashley's actually claim to have had some sort of spiritual experience that they speak of after waking from coma. It's as though a window has been opened to such patients. However, the window is only open for a time. Eventually, it closes. Therefore, you might want to make note of these discussions that you share with your daughter." The conversations that Ashley and I shared were interesting, heartfelt, as well as sometimes very emotional. Therefore, I decided to make a special appointment for Ashley to meet with her youth pastor also, to gain insight from a trusted Christian mentor.

During our conference, Pastor Ken's reaction to Ashley's testimony was similar to mine, which was that of complete awe. Yet, humbling to say the least. He smiled, concluding that Ashley reminded him of the "apostle Paul," a character in the New Testament who claimed to have visited heaven and returned, and who later wrote that he had witnessed things that he couldn't disclose. Ashley politely smiled at the youth pastor and nodded her head. I concurred, while advising him, that after Ashley started to pull out of coma and started writing about communing with Jesus, I had asked her a few questions that she had matter-of-factly advised that I was not supposed to ask, "as though Jesus had instructed her, while they were communing, to not answer specific questions." I then advised the youth pastor about the statistics the neurologist had informed me of relating to the subject of supernatural beings. I smiled when I told him, "Eighty percent is a very high number of individuals reporting to have had some form of a supernatural experience with God." He and I both found that information absolutely fascinating.

Jacob was absolutely awesome with his sister's homecoming. He was only four years of age at the time, and so he was definitely too young to assist with the basic tasks associated with his eldest sister's care. However, it was clear he was compassionate and eagerly wanted to help in any way he could. Oftentimes, he thoughtfully requested to assist with pushing her in her wheelchair while other times, Jacob opted to selflessly help with Ashley's recreational activities without even being asked. For instance, he'd place a movie in the DVD player of her personal television set in her bedroom, grab the remote, and then climb into Ashley's hospital bed right next to her. He then would start the film for the two of them, and then ring the dinner bell, summoning my undivided attention. Once I was within sight of the doorway, he'd say, "Mommy, Ashley wants a snack and something to drink. And..." He'd pause for a moment and look over at his sister before continuing with, "Ashley wants you to bring me a snack and a drink too." Then they'd both giggle mischievously. Once they had their snacks, the film started. Now the other amusing thing about this is that during that time, because of his age, Jacob often selected to view animated films with his eldest sister, to the extent that on one occasion, Ashley wrote on her notebook paper, "How old am I?!!!" I answered, "You're nineteen." And then I explained, "Jacob's only four years old. He enjoys watching films created for his age group." She nodded her head to convey understanding. I speculate his last recollection of Ashley before her collision was that was her means of entertaining him when she'd help with watching over her younger siblings.

Essentially, Jacob truly displayed unconditional love and respect for Ashley through his random acts of kindness. He was a good brother. As they both grew older, Jacob grew stronger. Eventually he would grow and be capable to selflessly lift her 100-pound wheelchair into the back of our vehicle as an attempt to help me, without being asked. Other times, Jacob would offer to push Ashley in her wheelchair while we were out in town; whether we were at church, at the store shopping, or attending a public event. The thoughtfulness and assistance that Jacob displayed at such a young age, trying to be useful, speaks volumes about my son's good character, and it was a characteristic that was frequently commended and not discouraged. However, running with and then popping a wheelie with Ashley's wheelchair, while she was sitting in it, certainly was discouraged and not recommended! That's about the only thing that Jacob would attempt on a routine occasion that truly both frightened and perplexed Ashley from time to time. In those moments, Ashley would convey discord toward her playful younger sibling. I'd respond, "What do you expect? He's the little brother and...a very adventurous boy child." During those moments, I'd have to keep a very close eye on my rambunctious son, gently scolding him to not scare his sister. He would mind, while giggling.

Ariel was instrumental with Ashley's care, offering much needed relief to me as I tended to other responsibilities and tasks, and especially during moments when I simply needed alone time. Having understood the incredible strides her sister had made in recovery, she lovingly disclosed to her silly sister, "Ashley, you are my favorite superhero. You are so strong."

A few years later, Ariel graduated from high school with high honors and was nominated for college scholarships. However, during her last few years of high school, she also had received basic nurses' training from me, as a result of helping to provide care to her older sister at home. Having helped with her sister's care, this also made Ariel feel less helpless over Ashley's condition. Her assistance, and having to maturely cope with circumstances that most of her peers at school couldn't even fathom, speaks volumes about Ariel's good character.

After my niece Jasmine—Ashley's cousin and closest friend—completed high school, she was also very instrumental with Ashley's care, also having received training from me, before opting to go on to work at a skilled nursing facility. Jasmine eventually started a family of her own.

My mother—Ashley's grandmother—would assist with tending to Ashley on occasion, also.

Eventually, I hired skilled home health caregivers through an agency. However, we learned that finding a good, hardworking, trustworthy, reliable employee wasn't easy. The average home health caregiver who was referred to us through an outside agency usually lasted about three months. However, a few of them were fearful of my spouse and preferred being scheduled during times when he wasn't home. Jason complained a lot. He was always changing the terms of what he thought would make him happier. For example, while Ashley was in the hospital, he complained about how much time I spent at the hospital. Once Ashley was home from the hospital, he complained about how much time I devoted to her care, insisting I hire help. Once I hired help, he would complain that he didn't want strangers in our home. It would appear that no matter what I did, he was forever changing the terms with regard to what he thought would make him happy. Meanwhile, his apathetic nature made being in his presence difficult.

I recall Ashley sitting at the kitchen table, smiling and greeting my spouse with a wave, once he returned from work. In return, Jason glared at her and didn't respond. Such moments were perplexing for me. I thought it was awesome that my daughter was trying to communicate. Yet, she discerned that my husband was being unnecessarily unkind.

I recall on one occasion when I was sitting next to Ashley, she finally reacted to her rude stepdad. She picked up her writing instrument and proceeded to write the word, "D!@K!" I concurred with her. I then removed the paper, so he wouldn't see what she had written. Suddenly, she angrily raised her righthand and made an unfavorable hand gesture, directed at Jason. Fortunately, he had his back to us and didn't see his stepdaughter's abrupt, offensive, universal sign language. I quickly lowered Ashley's hand at the very moment he turned around. And there both Ashley and I were, as he glanced back at us. Ashley looking "angry," as though winding up for a confrontation. And me looking "guilty" as a result of concealing her discord as means to prevent a confrontation. Once he left the room, I advised Ashley that I understood her upset, yet I asked her to refrain from using unfavorable hand gestures.

In one regard, I think it's amazing that she made an accurate assessment, as helpless as she was. However, in the same regard, I think Jason could've been a lot more empathetic, patient, and kind, as well as more of a loving parental role model within her life, since he was her stepdad at the time. He made it clear he had his favorites, although he was completely aware of what Ashley had survived. At no point did Jason ever participate in assisting with Ashley's care. He never even attempted to lift a spoon to her mouth to help feed her. He wouldn't even help with pushing her in her wheelchair during family public gatherings.

What's more, I think Jason could've been a better husband and more sensitive to my emotions and placed less strain on the family. I was thankful he at least constructed a wheelchair ramp and implemented a few renovations as well as modifications to our former residence.

Nonetheless, Ashley needed me more.

Recreational Therapy

One of the first things I noted during outings with Ashley is that not all places have wheelchair access. I never noticed such things before my eldest daughter became disabled. However, trying to find someone to help lift Ashley up or down a flight of stairs wasn't always easy. And trying to find a handicapped parking space is extremely problematic sometimes. What's more, Ashley's wheelchair wasn't equipped with all-terrain wheels. It's strenuous to maneuver her wheelchair through gravel, sod, or snow, and it's quite literally impossible to roll across a sand-covered beach. Therefore, pushing her wheelchair up as well as over a hilly terrain is more exerting then one would presume. Fortunately, there are a few lakes and beaches within the United States that have all-terrain wheelchairs (aka "sand wheelchairs") available for day use on beach premises. However, such wheelchairs become buoyant very easily once they are placed into a body of water. Therefore, it's important to practice caution while using such contraptions. Ambulating Ashley into as well as out of a vehicle during extreme weather conditions, such as during a rain, snow, or hailstorm, is simply distressing for both of us. Keeping the seat cushions dry, while trying to move Ashley, during the rain or a snowstorm was quite literally impossible with our means of transportation. After she sits down in her chair during a storm, I'm sure it's temporarily uncomfortable for her. However, staying active is important. I've learned to carry a towel or blanket in my vehicle, along with many other items I never dreamed of having to bring along.

That being said, a short time after Ashley was discharged from the hospital, I treated my children, as well as a neighboring family, to a trip to the Disneyland theme park. My family had visited the theme park on countless occasions. Yet, this would be the first time we visited the park with an individual who was severely disabled. And the other family accompanying us had never visited the theme park at all.

I was impressed with the attentiveness of the theme park's employees. There were a few rides equipped to accommodate individuals confined to wheelchairs. Ashley enjoyed the *Small World* boat ride the most. The first time through, Ashley was rocking out while aboard the boat to the theme song music. She was sort of mildly head-banging to the beat of the song, while obnoxiously waving her right hand in the air, signing "I love you." We were laughing so hard upon seeing Ashley's actions aboard the boat ride. The Disneyland attendants on that particular ride were equally amused. In such a manner, they opted to put our boat through a second time without even being asked. Afterward, I graciously thanked their staff for making Ashley's day to the Disneyland theme park so enjoyable.

On another occasion, I treated my children out to Sea World. They really liked the dolphin aquarium. They were actually hopeful I'd have a similar aquarium installed in our residence so that they, too, could swim around in it.

My children enjoy their beach as well as their swimming pool excursions. However, we soon learned Ashley doesn't tolerate being in the sunlight for a prolonged period of time. She has a very fair complexion. Therefore, we had to limit our time or go later in the day, for such family outings or simply find places to visit that offered plenty of shade as well as air conditioning.

Attending Faith-Based Events

At home, Ashley sat quietly with her notepad and a writing instrument, within the parameters of our residence, listening to Christian radio. She memorized the names of the bands and the songs, oftentimes lip-syncing along as a form of Speech Therapy and entertainment. She listened intently, jotting down broadcasted Christian concert information from time to time. One afternoon, Ashley scribbled the concert information on her notepad, with the simple request, "Take me to this concert." Attending faith-based events wasn't anything new to our family, and so I brought Ashley and both of her siblings to the outdoor music concert as she had requested.

The place was crowded, and seeing the stage was difficult. However, we enjoyed attending the concert nonetheless. After the concert, we started to make our way through the crowd and back to where I had parked my vehicle, when all of a sudden, Ashley grasped the right wheel of her wheelchair and demanded (using sign language) to meet the band. At that moment, due to the crowd, I wasn't sure if we'd have the opportunity to meet with the members of the band or not. Nonetheless, we made our way back into the concert area and decided to head toward the direction of the souvenir table. Once we arrived at the table, Ashley selected a band poster, and we did meet a few of the members. I shared her testimony with the band, and they seemed intrigued. My children and I left there that evening having enjoyed the concert, the time of fellowship, and also happy to have met Ashley's simple, adamant request to meet the band.

Vacation

Once I felt Ashley was strong enough to travel longer distances, we ventured out of state to visit family and friends. We had a nice gathering at her former place of employment in the Midwest among family, friends, and her former colleagues. There she met up with the two men who had proposed marriage to her while she was in the hospital. She even kissed one of them. Jody opted to meet us out at the shopping mall to treat Ashley to a shopping excursion. I recall the two of them sniffing perfumes together and then later comparing their scars, each with their own independent scar stories. Jody took it upon himself to attempt to show both Ashley and I how to work the *word predict* feature on her communication device.

A third friend of hers, Anthony, simply sat there crying while staring at her. He was politely smiling at both of us, thankful she had survived. Ashley and all of her friends, at the time, were children on the brink of adulthood, in their late teens. Intermingling with them, I perceived that the news about Ashley being in a vehicle collision and her hospitalization was almost too difficult for their young minds to bear. This was true for Ariel, who was five years younger than they were. Certainly I could empathize with their depression. It was difficult for them to see a once-athletic Ashley confined to a wheelchair. Yet, I know they were glad that Ashley recognized each of them and to see she had survived the catastrophe. And I know a few of them went on to become educated as well as employed within the field of health care. During that particular visit we made to the Midwest, Ashley's friend Teesha took her out for a few hours for a girls' night out.

That year, we traveled to visit relatives as far as the state of New York. Ashley's uncle Skip had a discussion with her about her visit to heaven. Their discussion reduced him to tears also. She had gifted him and his family with one of the crosses she had painted.

Day Spa Outings

Back in southern California, my children and I had visited a salon on a regular basis for an array of different services. On one occasion, I learned Ashley's friend Erica had become employed there, and so I scheduled a surprise visit for each of them. On the day of the appointment, when Erica saw Ashley, she started sobbing. Ashley hugged Erica, trying to comfort her once-best friend, as she wept. "Ashley, you're so strong," Erica said. Upsetting Erica that day certainly wasn't intended.

Unconditional Love Amidst Adversity

I filed for divorce in 2006. At first, my children were alright with my decision, although in the divorce proceedings, I lost the majority of my investments and I had to relocate my family. During that time, I encountered much opposition from relatives, friends, and acquaintances once they learned that I had filed for divorce. The harsh criticism was almost too much to bear. Nonetheless, I still moved on with my life. I don't regret making that decision.

"Pete"

One Sunday afternoon in 2008, after leaving church and shortly after getting settled in to a rental home, on the outskirts of town, God blessed my family once again.

I had been without my own transportation. However, I had finally managed to save up enough funds to put a down payment on a used vehicle—a gold-colored Ford F150 XLT—after taking the vehicle on a test-drive with a Christian car salesman. After the test drive, he and I placed our hands on the hood of the vehicle and prayed. Within six hours, I had the keys in hand, the vehicle insured, and I proceeded to pull out of the dealership parking lot in route to my residence.

Once I pulled into the driveway of my residence, both Ariel and Jacob ran outside, cheering. They were ecstatic that I was capable of purchasing a vehicle, perfect for our now-small family of four.

Shortly after I purchased the truck, my zealous son Jacob, seven years old at the time, helped me affix a Christian cross applique on the back window, designed by a popular Christian clothing vendor NOTW (an acronym inspired by Jesus' words from the book of John 17:16, *"They are not of this world, even as I am not of this world."*) I advised Jacob, "God has been very good to our family." Jacob concurred.

My children know that over the course of time, I ended up naming the truck after an established male Christian musician from Australia, as a result of listening to a lot of the vintage songs he and his band composed together. Hence, the name "Pete."

Ariel graduated from high school in 2009. She went on to attend college and complete her studies in southern California. Meanwhile, shortly after Ariel's high school graduation, I relocated what was left of my small family to the state of New York in 2009, with a single divorce court case pending in the state of California.

We arrived with three suitcases. Both Ashley and I required medical attention and were evaluated. Ashley experienced a grand mal seizure. I collapsed from stress overload after weeks of being "hypervigilant." I still remember my dad standing over me, telling me that I needed medical treatment, while I was on the hospital gurney, preparing to stand up. So, there in the emergency department, Ashley and I were side by side in an observation room, with fluids being administered to each of us intravenously.

Ashley lay in the gurney next to mine, not moving, not responding, simply staring off into nowhere. It was similar to how she had been upon first emerging from coma. We were both released from the hospital, once the seizure symptoms had worn off and she became responsive. However, the seizure Ashley had experienced caused her to lose the abilities she had gained to her right side. Essentially, she regressed. The seizure diminished her ability to write as well as feed herself. She couldn't draw fluid through a straw anymore, and she could no longer drink fluids from a cup. Therefore, to keep her hydrated, I opted to administer fluids to her, orally, through means of a plastic-tip medical irrigation syringe instead of a baby bottle. To keep her nourished, I had to spoon-feed every meal to her, foods at a pureed consistency. The care she required became equivalent to that of having an infant child. It was upsetting to see her lose the abilities she had gained back. However, I'm thankful we both survived that ordeal.

Within a few weeks, we got settled into an apartment with the help of a few folks, both churchgoers as well as non-churchgoers. I had a pending divorce, out-of-state. Yet, my children and I were a "new" family in town, trying to do our best in starting over after moving across the continent.

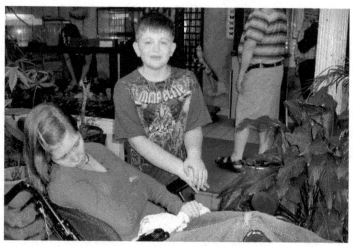

Ashley & Jacob at the Conservatory, 2010.

Within less than a year, I found temporary employment in a government career. However, after my assignment ended, it didn't take long to determine that our moving to the East Coast had not been a good move. At least, it had not been a good move for my family. In our experience, we found there were many citizens who didn't like Christians, some of whom, quite literally, would attempt to provoke an argument with either me or my son.

Jacob, at the tender age of nine, was perplexed, having never been subject of religious persecution until then. He ended up in a few arguments, as well as some fights. However, I recall that such adversity caused my son to draw closer to God, and it brought about many meaningful discussions pertaining to Christianity as well as our constitutional rights. Being the leader of the family, I did what I needed to do to protect my family. Nonetheless, I still remember the day when Ashley, Jacob, and I sat down at the kitchen table and took a unanimous vote to relocate back to the West Coast. We had had it! We were in a situation in which we didn't want to stay. However, neither could we afford to leave the state. We were struggling financially.

During the winter months, Jacob started shoveling snow to earn extra money. One of the first things he purchased was a small portable space heater, to ensure we wouldn't freeze to death after our furnace ran out of oil and while we were waiting for an oil delivery. Ashley, Jacob, and I slept that night in the same bedroom, with the doors closed, and we managed to stay warm throughout the entire evening. I was happy the oil delivery was made before Jacob returned home from school the next afternoon.

The day before Mother's Day that year, Jacob asked me to drive him to the store. He was ten years of age at the time, and he told he needed to do some shopping. Therefore, I drove him to a retail store in a neighboring town. Once we arrived, he told me to wait in the truck with Ashley. So, I allowed my handsome ten-year-old son to walk into the store alone while I sat in my vehicle, waiting in the parking lot. I knew Jacob was up to something. He returned a few minutes later and told me to cover my eyes and not peek. We returned home, and Jacob disappeared into his room with his purchases.

The next morning, Jacob woke up early. He looked at me and said, "Happy Mother's Day. Don't get out of bed." Moments later, Jacob returned with a tray and a breakfast that he had prepared all by himself. On the tray were two roses, as well as two homemade greeting cards—one from him, as well as one from Ashley. As I sat there in bed, staring at the breakfast tray, I thought, *I am blessed with a wonderful son. He is such a wonderful brother to Ashley. He selflessly put this together without any prompting from me.* I thanked Jacob for being so thoughtful.

While we discussed saving funds with the intent to eventually relocate back to a warmer climate, we opted to relocate to a different township in the meantime. Jacob started attending a new school before the school year had ended, and he became friends with a few new acquaintances his age. For encouragement, I'd read daily Christian devotionals to my son while we were waiting at the bus stop, before sending him off to school. Once he was off to school, I'd then turn my attention over to tending to Ashley.

However, within three weeks after we relocated and got settled into our new residence and the new school district, my ex-husband visited the state of New York and decided to abduct Jacob. Then he absconded from the state of New York with him, after lying to the local police department. Meanwhile, my request for an "Immediate Relief Order" for an Amber Alert from the court was disregarded, during the first rescue attempt. For over five weeks I was distraught, I grieved relentlessly, and I prayed. I wondered how my son was coping. I wondered if he was scared. I wondered if he found access to a wireless device or a landline telephone, if he would courageously attempt to notify me.

Ashley was very sorrowful also. She missed her brother. She could hear me sobbing each day. She understood the seriousness of the situation and my distress. She overheard the telephone conversations that I had with the police department, the courthouse, as well as relatives. My ex-husband had committed a very serious offense but he couldn't be bothered. I thought, *How could he do this to both Jacob and me?!!! How could he do this to the family?*

Five weeks later, once court was in session, immediately I was subject of religious persecution. I didn't appreciate the fact that there were those in the courtroom who were insensitive, trying to deviate from the matter of the abduction.

Nonetheless, after court adjourned, I drove out to the center of a farmer's field on the outskirts of town and sobbed to the extent of being near speechless, while Ashley sat quietly in the cabin of my truck, listening to my telephone conversation with my mother. Shortly thereafter, despite the fact that my heart was breaking and I was distraught from grief, I stood up on stage and still sang a praise and worship song in front of a mixed crowd. My daughter Ashley sat in the audience. As I sang onstage, my heart was breaking in front of that entire crowd. The majority of the audience didn't even know it.

That evening, I prayed, and through the means of the Holy Spirit, God comforted me with this scripture from the book of Matthew 5:10: *"Blessed are they which are persecuted for righteousness' sake: for theirs is the kingdom of heaven."*

Ashley wearing angel wings.

About three weeks later, Hurricane Irene, as well as Tropical Storm Lee, decided to touch down in the county in which we lived. Things went from bad to much worse in a short period of time. Roadways were swept away with the current. Other access streets were closed. The courthouse and the sheriff's department were flooded, along with countless homes and businesses. Hundreds of citizens had to evacuate their residences and take refuge in a temporary shelter.

Ashley and I were fortunate that our residence, built on higher ground, had not been affected by the storms, and at no point did we lose power. Countless other folks weren't as fortunate. Therefore, I opted to jump into "Pete" (my truck) and show up at the fire department to ask the chief if they needed my volunteer service.

During the next few hours, Ashley accompanied me, while I utilized my own resources during the rescue and relief efforts. We hauled and delivered supplies to the designated shelters, everything from food to bed cots. And wouldn't you have guessed it...while the state of New York made national news, in a state of emergency, my ex-husband was traveling in route to the state of New York with Jacob, with the intent to appear for a court appointment, and he finally decided to answer his wireless device and opted to argue with me about the weather. We were arguing about both the weather as well as finances. At the time, he thought I was lying to him over the phone about the storms and the massive flooding. I pleaded with him to turn his vehicle around, since he was traveling with my son. I advised him to either tune in to the radio-broadcasted news or to stop somewhere to view the televised news. He insisted on being belligerent. Therefore, I advised him to heed the soldiers of the National Guard in the event he pulled up to a road closure. I'm not sure what my ex-husband did next after he hung up the phone.

The weeks that followed found Ashley and me traveling all over upstate New York in order to distribute government forms and supplies to the farmers, small business owners, and countless families who had fallen victim to the horrific floods.

Participating in such outreach ministry, while redirecting our attention from our preexisting important matters, was in some ways complicated for me. I silently prayed that my son was alright. There were times when I volunteered alongside soldiers of the National Guard and moments when I worked independently. We truly were attempting to make a positive difference in the middle of the crisis, with the intent to encourage newfound hope for several souls who were emotionally devastated after being displaced from their homes or losing their businesses and were unemployed as a result of the flood. Oftentimes Ashley rode along with me.

Once court resumed, despite my noble efforts, I was mocked, discriminated against, and criticized due to the fact that I provided care to a loved one with a severe disability. Ashley sat in on most of those unjust court hearings and trials. She was equally outraged over what the other attorneys were saying. Yet, Ashley couldn't defend herself verbally. I was distraught, struggling to hold my composure, and baffled over the events as well as the acts of injustice and aggravated depression. It all seemed so surreal and unfair. Needless to say, I eventually got into a few fueled arguments after court had adjourned with a couple of those attorneys.

As a mother, conservator, advocate, personal assistant, and caregiver who was familiar with the regular day-to-day stressors associated with providing care to a loved one with a disability, the act of unwelcome frequent adversity leads to only two things...depleting one's strength and causing anxiousness. As believers, we aren't supposed to be anxious about anything (see Philippians 4:6). Amidst the court proceedings, I simply expected everyone to do their job as professionally and as expediently as possible. Those within a position of authority failed miserably, and the court case was handled as though it was a big joke to them, almost stealing every ounce of hope from me.

However, I was fortunate that at least the family court judge ordered Jacob be allowed to visit the state of New York during the month of December that year. The judge ordered that my former spouse and I split Jacob's time off from school during the winter break. The judge ordered that I cover the expense of a one-way ticket to the state of New York for my son and delegated my former spouse to cover the expense of a one-way ticket for him back to the Midwest. I chose the dates when Jacob could visit during Christmas. With me as the petitioner, I didn't concur with the judge entirely. However, in good faith, I upheld his order. I didn't think I should've been expected to return Jacob to his dad, considering the ill manner in which he had been removed from the state of New York in the first place. I figured, during that time, that the courthouse employees and attorneys could've made themselves more useful and consulted with the local district attorney's office in order to prosecute my ex-husband along with his accomplice(s) so that Jacob could be returned to me and not have to worry about returning to the Midwest. However, that didn't occur. Nonetheless, I upheld the court order, trying to display to both the courts and my son that I knew how to follow the rules. As frustrated as I was at the time, I still tried to be the role model and the "good example" for the sake of my son.

Christmastime

I had the house decorated for Christmas by the time Jacob arrived on Friday, December 23, 2011. That afternoon, I showed up at the Albany airport wearing angel wings. I walked through the airport corridors and straight to the gate where Jacob would be arriving. My ten-year-old son sort of smirked at me the moment he spotted me standing there with the angel wings on. We returned to our residence. That evening, after dinner and after getting Ashley settled in for the night, Jacob and I stayed up to listen to a church service, via the internet, from our former home church out in the state of California. The living room was illuminated by only the Christmas lights on our Christmas tree and a computer screen. Jacob lay down on the love seat with his head on my lap and his legs over the armrest. Before the pastor was finished preaching, Jacob was sound asleep in a deep, peaceful rest. I stared at my son while he slept and thought, *He is such a momma's boy.* All of the tension we had both experienced, brought on during the previous months, seemed eliminated for a few moments, and things seemed as they should be. With the exception, Ariel wasn't there. She was busy out on the West Coast, attending her second year of college. I was thankful to be able to reach her by telephone so she could speak with the three of us during Jacob's visit.

On Christmas Day, after opening gifts and having a nice breakfast, Jacob noticed me preparing to bake a cake for Ashley's birthday. He stopped what he was doing to assist me in the kitchen, eventually taking over the cake project entirely while I started to prepare

Christmas dinner. We enjoyed the week that we spent together as a family. Before the New Year rang in, it was time to send Jacob back to his dad. That was the last Christmas both Ashley and I shared with Jacob while he was still a child. Had I known I wouldn't see him again until he was thirteen, I think I would've hugged him a little bit longer before allowing him to board the aircraft.

Springtime

I'd been in and out of court and received a bad verdict from the judge. Devastated, I opted to appeal his decision. Trying to find a resolution wasn't happening fast enough. I was searching for gainful employment while Ashley resumed attending a day program for a few hours, five days a week. When I wasn't out looking for work, I'd go out on hiking/caving excursions for exercise and to clear my mind.

I love how Jesus met up with both Ashley and me during our depression, on Easter weekend in 2012. I sat at the kitchen table reading out loud from holy Scripture, pertaining to the resurrection of Jesus Christ. Ashley sat up in her hospital bed in the next room, listening intently. Moments after I finished reading, I heard a rustling noise in the room where Ashley was.

Nonchalantly, I turned around to glance over into the room, and I did a double take. Much to my surprise, at the foot of Ashley's bed appeared the apparition of a man, dressed in white linen. His brown hair was about shoulder length. His skin color was tan. His eye color was dark brown. He stood there smiling and then nodded, as though He was proud of me. I stood up, silently, staring back into the face of the One who I believe is my Savior. I wasn't frightened. However, I have no idea how long He was standing there. Tears of joy filled my eyes and rolled down my face. Within a few seconds, the apparition slowly disappeared. I walked over close to where I had seen the apparition standing and asked Ashley, "Did you see that?" I looked over at her, and she was staring at the precise area where the apparition had stood. Ashley nodded. She didn't look frightened, either. However, we both were in awe that evening. I'm thankful we experienced that sighting together. I notified a few members of the clergy, via the internet, to give a testimony pertaining to that extraordinary sighting. Since then, I've placed this scripture in Ashley's bedroom: *"Blessed are the pure in heart: for they shall see GOD"* (Matthew 5:8).

A few months later, I was sitting outdoors on the patio, late one night. As I sat there, I noticed it was very foggy outdoors. The clouds seemed to be hanging very low within the neighborhood. In such a way, I noticed a cloud in the corner, sort of nestled underneath the overhead balcony eaves, a polite distance from where I was sitting. I glanced back over at the cloud overhead and pondered how odd it was, hovering in the corner. I stood up to walk into my residence. The vapor cloud moved suddenly, slowly unveiling a cloak of wings, revealing a cherubim, about the size of a small toddler child, hidden in disguise. The encounter was similar to that of watching a floral bud open. The cherubim, a white fog in color, hovering there, turned around and looked at me as though I had awakened it from rest. Yet, it showed me that it had the ability to defy gravity. There wasn't any video projector equipment in the area, projecting prerecorded graphics of someone's interpretation of what a cherubim would look like. What I seen that evening was from the spirit realm. I was wide-eyed and startled. In my mind, I was yelling, "Ahhhhhhhhh-hhhhhhhhhhhhhhhh!" Yet I didn't yell out loud. Instead, I stood up, quietly and quickly, walking back into my residence and closing the door. In that moment, I was reminded of the angelic encounters of those in holy Scripture, where an angel says, "Fear not." They meant, "Do not fear," or rather, "Do not be troubled." I speculate that, more than likely, those documented in holy Scripture as having a close encounter with an angelic being were initially frightened. Such things are rare occurrences, not something that happens every day. I'm thankful that I believe in a God who doesn't limit Himself to what is archived within the pages of holy Scripture. I believe God sent that cherubim, initially disguised as a cloud, to check in on us that evening, perhaps even to guard us, aware of the *reality* of the oppression to which we had been subjected. And while that encounter was unexpected, it was still quite amazing. I speculate that what I saw that evening might have been similar to that of what Ashley had described seeing, days before she was in her vehicle collision.

A few months later, a handsome man with whom I wasn't acquainted found me in the village one afternoon during a rainstorm. His name was John. He asked me to sit down with him in his vehicle. I'm not accustomed to getting into a vehicle with a stranger. However, as I stood outside of John's vehicle, I noted an image of the archangel Michael on the side of his sedan. He sat calmly in the driver's seat with a fist full of prayer cards. He disclosed he wasn't from the area and advised that he'd like to speak with me. In good faith, I opened the passenger-side door and sat down in the front passenger seat of his vehicle. John identified himself as a member of the Catholic religion and then asked if I had experienced any sightings of angels. I'm not a Catholic.

However, I *am* a Christian. At first, I was apprehensive to answer John's question and sort of giggled nervously. During that brief conversation, I confessed to him that I had experienced a few sightings. However, I also informed John that "my mother doesn't like me talking about such encounters." John smiled without making any eye contact with me and busied himself with wiping the droplets of rain off of the interior side panel of his driver's-side door, with a bandanna. During our conversation, he made reference to a word in the Greek language. He then handed me a prayer card with an illustration of the archangel Michael preparing to slay the beast. He dismissed me from that discussion. I got out of his vehicle, closed the door, and proceeded on with my day. I do not know if John studies books about angels, if he is employed through the church that he attends, or if he was some sort of researcher pertaining to sightings from the spiritual realm. John and I didn't exchange telephone numbers or addresses to stay in communication with one another. However, based upon the discussion as well as his curiosity, I'd suggest he has a reverence for such heavenly beings and perhaps experienced a personal encounter at some point, also.

I relocated to the outskirts of town. Paranormal activity continued to occur on occasion. Jokingly, I referred to such encounters as "Polter-guests". Some things can't be explained. I prayed to God while trying to seek out the answers. I was wondering what He was trying to teach me during that particular stage of my life. I'd been aware of spiritual warfare as articulated in holy Scripture for years. I was sober. I wasn't taking any sort of prescription medication or illicit substances. I wasn't participating in, nor reading books associated with, any occult religion. And...I didn't want to attend secular counseling and risk being assessed by an atheist.

Therefore, eventually I met up with and spoke to a bishop from the Orthodox Christian Church pertaining to the subject of angel beings and paranormal activity. The church bishop advised me that angel sightings are rare and oftentimes are interpreted as a "special calling" for those of who experience such encounters within the family of Jesus Christ. Our conversation enlightened me. Shortly after that time, both Ashley and I were invited to stay at a monastery as guests for a while. Yet, we didn't participate in the women's retreat at the monastery.

Jacob, W.L. Adams & Ashley in 2014.

Needless to say, it took seven years to finally resolve my divorce. I don't wish any ill will toward my former spouse. I hope that he's a happier man, regardless what he believes or disbelieves. What I know is that I love my children and that'll never change.

A comical moment is the conversation I shared with a male acquaintance from a different Christian church, regarding the subject of the paranormal. He sarcastically mused, "Hey, Wen, if you keep talking about ghosts, spirits, angels, and demons, the guys in the white lab coats are going to want to subject you to shock therapy." I responded, "Well then, if that is so, I'd refuse treatment."

I Believe in Angels

When I was a child, my paternal grandparents oftentimes would assist with providing care to my eldest sister and me, as both of our parents were employed. My grandmother was a retired secretary from a local school, within the small town in which I currently reside, while my grandfather retired from a local nursing home. Both of my grandparents were actively involved within the community and were instrumental in assisting with my sister's and my upbringing. Their residence always represented a safe haven to me. It was a place where I learned to pray and could enthusiastically discuss my hopes, dreams, and aspirations. It was a place where I truly felt loved.

In 2016, I was still struggling with symptoms of aggravated depression. Both Ashley and I were suffering from financial hardship. I missed my two youngest children immensely, and I hadn't heard from them in some time. I felt shipwrecked emotionally, defeated, and perfectly miserable. Tending to Ashley's care was the only thing that gave me motivation to get out of bed and face each day. I felt as though I couldn't relax. I was on guard, bracing myself for the next unexpected problem to confront. I felt isolated from society. I was an introvert within a crowd. Most of the people in the town seemed angry, harsh, and unwelcoming. Therefore, I busied myself with painting, writing, photography, and making bouquets out of wildflowers. During that time, as both Ashley and I lived in the heart of a forest, God amazed me with wildlife that He would send to visit me to cheer me up. Specifically, there was one chipmunk that visited regularly and would scurry around my feet, looking for a snack, while I'd be sitting out on the back patio. God knew I was silently grieving. God knew, aside from all the other conflicts, my greatest of concerns was Ashley's health appeared to be slowly deteriorating, despite my efforts.

Several years before, she had lost a lot of weight, for reasons unbeknownst to us. She had depleted to an alarming 70 pounds, and she appeared gaunt and frail. I had spent several years trying to get her to maintain and gain weight. Yet, she didn't seem to gain an ounce. She was no longer attending a day rehabilitation program and home with me full-time, again, enabling me to better monitor her nutritional needs as well as her environment. As much as I was concerned over Ashley's health, I struggled with my own emotions, devastated by relatives who caused me to feel as though my daughter and I had been ostracized from the family. I was frustrated with friends and former colleagues. At that point, my dating life was also practically extinct.

One October afternoon, I ventured into the village to run errands. Both Ashley and I decided to visit a historic home (the DAR building) while the building structure subject of the hurricane floods was undergoing massive renovation, in the village of Schoharie. The admirable renovation project was close to completion. Yet, as I stood alone in an upstairs room that was awaiting its restoration, suddenly I felt as though someone else had entered the room. I turned around. Yet, no one was there. I thought, *How odd.* I left the building with Ashley expediently. I decided to head in the direction of my grandparents' former residence; A historic colonial style farm house built in the 19th Century, neighboring a couple farms and set on over 200 acres of rolling hills and bare land, encompassed by natural forest areas, with a fishing reservoir in the backyard. That autumn day, as we traveled out to a neighboring town and then down the street of where that house is located, I was ecstatic to discover that the property was vacated. Immediately, I notified the property owner to inquire if I could rent the property. He said, "Yes." Therefore, I placed an immediate move-out notice to the property owner whom I had been renting from and started packing right away.

The previous tenants of the property to which we were relocating had left the place in ruins, in comparison to how my grandparents had kept up the property during their time there. The historic home required much work, including extensive cleaning along with renovations. I walked the exterior of the property, before move-in, making notes of the damages that the property owner would need to address. Then, I pulled out a small bottle of anointing oil and blessed the house.

Once Ashley and I received the keys to the historic house in which my grandparents used to reside, we were overjoyed. Over the years, Ashley and my other two children had heard countless stories of my childhood memories created there.

The evening Ashley and I moved into that house, the power was on. Yet, it was dark. I lost my stainless-steel scripture ring right around the time of replacing a light bulb in an overhead light fixture. Ashley patiently waited in my truck in the driveway, until I managed to get the lighting on indoors. Once I had the lights turned on, I returned to my vehicle, reached into the cabin of my truck, scooped Ashley up into my arms, and carried her frail body into the home. I still had a lot of unpacking to do, as well as a hospital bed to set up. At the time, I truly believed it was a good move.

That first night, sleeping in that house once again, reduced me to tears. I prayed out loud, with Ashley resting next to me in the same bed. I was so tired. Yet, I was so happy at the same time. I hadn't slept in that residence since I was a child. I felt like I was finally home.

One afternoon, my older sister Lisa and her fiancée decided to visit, and they brought a pizza dinner with them. My sister didn't walk any part of the house alone. However, we enjoyed dinner together. They could see there was a lot of work to be done. And we were fortunate they had visited.

During the weeks that followed, necessary maintenance, repairs, and renovations were addressed, assisting with redirecting my frustration. I tended to Ashley, while also deep-cleaning the entirety of the residence, unpacking storage containers, planning the course of the renovations, and eventually cleaning up the surrounding yard. The projects were coming along nicely. During the day, we'd listen to Christian songs over the stereo.

Shortly, after we moved into the residence, one afternoon I was standing in the kitchen unpacking and trying to get settled in. I was startled, suddenly, upon one of the front doors abruptly swinging open, slamming into the wall as though an excited guest had just arrived to visit. And yet it appeared no one was standing in the doorway, at all. I logically reasoned that it was probably the wind. Yet, I noted the other door had not opened in the same manner.

While I was cleaning that three-story residence and unpacking, moving household furniture items into their usual rooms was temporarily postponed. Therefore, I set my bed up in the living room on one level. Most of the nights were quiet and peaceful. Yet the very night after I'd finally finished getting Ashley's hospital bed set up in the room in which she would be sleeping, I was awakened abruptly that night. I opened my eyes and saw an angel walk through the living room and then through the adjacent wall from where I was sleeping, bringing my attention directly to the shape of a translucent heart painted on the wall. I hadn't noticed that image before then, and it was difficult to see, except at that specific angle. As I lay there in my bed, staring at that heart image painted on the wall, I felt a sense of heartwarming joy and amazement. I felt a tear roll down my cheek, and I slowly fell to sleep. The next morning, once I determined the vision I had wasn't just a dream, I happily painted a square around the heart-shaped image and captured an image of it with my digital camera before covering that wall in a few coats of fresh mocha-colored paint.

Several days later, I removed a panel in the residence and found the words, "I love you" painted underneath. I smiled upon seeing the welcoming words of love. I captured several before-and-after images with my camera amidst the renovations to show the property owner the progress that I and a hired male construction worker (also of the Christian faith) were making. Yet I also captured images of some of the other things I discovered along the way.

One evening, Ashley was sound asleep on the other side of the house while I busied myself in the kitchen. As I stood up from the table to get myself something to drink, the kitchen cabinet door with a magnetic closing mechanism where I stored the glassware opened on its own accord. Or rather, it was as though an invisible being, a very good host, had opened the cabinet door for me. I took a deep breath, slowly walked across the room, reached in the cupboard to retrieve a glass, slowly closed the cabinet door, and proceeded to get myself something to drink.

That December, I started a fund-raiser decorating and selling Christmas wreaths with the intention to build a wheelchair ramp on our residence. One evening, as I opened the door to the front porch to place a few orders outside, I saw an angel resembling my grandfather, as though he was passively walking in from outside. The angel spoke to me and disappeared as quickly as it had appeared. Had the angel been in a mortal body, we would've gently brushed shoulders. We were standing that close to one another. Yet in that moment, I thanked God for allowing me to experience such a vision. However, I was suddenly reduced to tears and I sat on the floor with my back up against the formal dining room wall. As I sat there, I reminisced of times past spent within that wonderful home, time well invested with my grandparents during the Christmas season.

Without a doubt, I know the angels were of God because they communicated love. Yet, oftentimes in my prayers at night and throughout the day, I'd ask God what their purpose was. The encounters I noted weren't imaginary or exaggerated. The visions didn't occur every day and were rather sporadic. I wasn't self-medicating with prescriptive medication or illicit substances, which cause hallucinations. I wasn't participating in any acts of witchcraft or the occult, because I already know those things weren't of God, according to Galatians 5:20.

Nonetheless, several months later, once I completed painting the formal dining room, I placed a simple heartfelt message on the wall that read:

"FAMILY, where life begins and love never ends..."

In the springtime of 2018, I began to improve the aesthetics of the yard. On occasion whitetail deer would meander into the yard. Sometimes I'd set out apple peelings for them to graze on, after making a home-made apple pie.

Other times, wild birds such as cardinals, blue jays, finches, sparrows, chickadees, and mourning doves would visit, perching themselves out on the birdfeeder filled with birdseed, located on the front porch.

One afternoon, I found a male painter turtle about the size of a quarter in the driveway. Because of his size and the wildlife out in that area, I decided to place him in an aquarium indoors and named the turtle Pebble. He was a special, unexpected blessing sent from God that brought both Ashley and me so much joy.

When I planted a beautiful garden alongside the en-tryway side of the home, Pebble would swim around in a plastic bowl that I set outdoors, close to where I was working. I'd have to keep an eye out for snakes, birds, and other larger creatures that might've tried to swal-low Pebble up in a single gulp. I was fortunate that Peb-ble stayed close and didn't wander off.

That spring, on the other side of the home, I trans-planted a few stems from one existing fragrant pink

rosebush and made a rose garden there. One afternoon, while I was on my knees, being mindful to weed-
ing the area, framing it in, then laying turf cover down
over the soil as well as mulch, I stopped to turn around
to reach for a few garden tools. Within a blink of an eye,
I was immediately surprised upon seeing a momentary
vision of an angel in the yard that resembled my grandmother. The vision appeared and then disappeared at
about the speed of light. Therefore, I decided to revere
the rose garden on the property in her memory.

Eventually, I planted a few strawberry plants in the
backyard. And then I learned that the property owners
had decided to place the property up for auction. Therefore, I tried to purchase the property in 2018, with the
intent to turn the surrounding acres into a Christmas
tree farm. My mother had only visited on one occasion
after I moved in, and she was so frustrated with me.
During a telephone discussion, she argued, "*You* are the
only individual in the family who wants to live there!"
I advised my mother, "That's not so. I'm not the only
individual who wants to live *here*."

Unfortunately, my statement to my mother rang
true the day of the auction, when I was outbid by $1,000.
Frustrated, I thought, "*Oh no!*" Even so, I had to prepare
once again to relocate Ashley and myself before the end
of the year. The last evening spent at that residence, I

sobbed so hard, not necessarily because of all the work I had done there over the course of two years, but because that place has such sentimental value to me. Having to move out of that place and into a smaller residence was absolutely heart-wrenching. However, I was grateful to have found alternate housing. And I have since learned the residence is now rented out as a vacation home.

During the time I had resided in that historic house, Ashley not only was diagnosed and hospitalized after the doctors had found she was suddenly stricken with E-coli, the intrathecal baclofen pump was surgically removed, and a stomach feeding tube was placed back into her abdomen. It was determined by a specialist that the feeding tube was necessary in order to assist Ashley with weight gain. After the feeding tube was placed, Ashley made great progress and finally started to gradually gain weight. In less than a year, she managed to meet and exceed the weight gain goal and finally weighed in at over 100 pounds again. I was thankful she had recovered from contracting E-coli and that she was on the upward spiral of returning to good health. However, the last few weeks we resided in that wonderful residence, it was found through means of radiograph imaging that Ashley also had an intestinal "obstruction" and required "emergency surgery." It was speculated by the surgeon that Ashley might've been born with such a defect. Therefore, he had to take her back to the operating room, without delay, to not only remove the obstruction but also to correct how her intestines were positioned. That surgeon saved Ashley's life. After her surgery, Ashley was hospitalized for the greater part of two weeks before being released to return home.

Irrefutably, while our visitors were few, what I learned between 2016 and 2018 is that most of the times when I experienced a sighting of one of those angelic messengers, Ashley had an unforeseen medical condition that needed to be addressed. God knew it. He knew something was overlooked that wasn't obvious. Yet, what a beautiful place God had returned me to, for a time, with Ashley: A place that was dear to me from the time of my youth. A place that represented a safe haven, a place of love, restoration, discovery, and where I first had learned about God. The very place my grandparents also provided care to me during the times I was sick with an infirmity as a child. And we stayed there for about two years in the wonder of it all.

Ashley and I relocated out of that historic home and into a newer residence a few weeks after her intestinal surgery was performed and she was released to return home from the hospital. Therefore, our plans of vacationing were temporarily postponed until I felt she would be strong enough to travel.

Ashley, 2016.

Girl Power!

During the year 2019, a huge milestone occurred within both Ashley's and my life. I turned fifty years of age, and I signed on with an agency that would compensate me for being a full-time personal assistant to Ashley. That enabled me, after ten years, to resume life with a steady income, effectively maintain a household, purchase a newer vehicle, and start planning for the future.

Later in the year, Ashley celebrated the fifteenth anniversary of surviving her vehicle collision. It was a huge milestone for her, that no one had ever expected back in 2004. Therefore, during the summer months, to celebrate, we decided to travel across the continent together, along with our pet turtle, Pebble, to visit Excalibur in Las Vegas, Nevada, visit relatives, as well as attend a Harvest Crusade at Angel Stadium, and visit Disneyland in southern California. It took us five days to drive to the state of California and another five days to return to upstate New York. We even had our theme colors selected—black and hot pink—along with a theme name for our cross-country adventure: our "Girl Power" excursion.

I invited my son, Jacob, since by this time he had completed high school and was planning to enlist within the United States Air Force. He had much to celebrate also. However, he left for training right around the time we set out en route for the West Coast.

On the way to California, we traveled through several rain and electrical storms. During our travels, we met quite a few interesting people and saw a few amazing sites we had never seen before. Ashley was in good spirits the entire time, and so was I.

I recall arriving on my mother's doorstep, late in the evening, with fresh flowers and a sack of food from a local Mexican restaurant. I was tired from driving over 2,800 miles, I was hungry, and I simply asked my mother if she'd be interested in attending the crusade with me and her granddaughter that weekend at Angel Stadium. My mother said, "No." She was disinterested in attending the crusade. In fact, she didn't seem at all happy to see us. She wasn't the least bit amused or surprised, but rather she appeared disgruntled by our surprise visit. This saddened and disappointed me. We stood there in the entryway for a few moments, conversing with one another. My mother sort of posed at the foot of the staircase as though guarding it and not permitting us entry to the second level of the residence. That might've been the point when I asked my mother where my older sister was. She advised me that everyone upstairs was sleeping and had to work the following day. Then she allowed both Ashley and me to sit down in the formal dining room for a few minutes so we could eat our late dinner before heading back out, en route to check into a motel.

The following day was much different. Ashley and I arrived at Angel Stadium on the second night of the crusade, well rested. That particular weekend Harvest Ministries was celebrating their thirtieth anniversary. We were so happy to be there for that event. The ushers warmly greeted us and gladly helped both Ashley and me to the section where they wanted us to be seated that night. There were thousands of people present in the stadium. Everyone was being kind and seemed ecstatic to also be there. As I stared out to the crowd that night, looking from the left to the right, there was an unmistakable, overwhelming, subtle reminder to myself: THIS is my "church family," the family of Jesus Christ. In that moment I felt very blessed to have arrived and made it there. However, as I silently glanced over at Ashley, I thought, I wish more of our blood relatives were here. Then I pondered, Is THIS what it's going to be like in *heaven?!!!* My heart was perplexed, rather *burdened*, for a moment. I'd never experienced that type of thought during a crusade before. I speculate it might have been the gentle prompting of Holy Spirit, persuading me to pray for my relatives.

My thoughts were abruptly refocused in a welcoming manner by a woman I wasn't acquainted with heading to the concession area. She smiled and offered to purchase a soda for me. I gladly accepted. Once the nice woman returned, she introduced me to her family. Her son had also survived a vehicle collision and was seated in his wheelchair right next to Ashley. We enjoyed fellowship with one another that evening. Before the night was through, her son had so much enjoyed meeting Ashley he decided that he wanted to generously purchase new T-shirts for both Ashley and me, a keepsake from the crusade event. We left the stadium that evening feeling enlightened. I treated Ashley out to dinner at a nearby restaurant before heading back to the motel room.

"Love One Another"

On the third day of our visit to the state of California, my mother asked both Ashley and me to stay at her home instead of the motel. Therefore, we decided to take my mother up on her offer. We showed up on the scene, Ashley wearing a T-shirt adorned with the simple message, "Love one another".

While we visited, I anxiously anticipated seeing my daughter Ariel (whom I hadn't seen in ten years). I was watching for her to arrive and walk through the front door. I anticipated throwing my arms around her and enjoying a long-overdue reunion with her and Ashley. However, I had been in the state of California for three days and hadn't heard even a word from Ariel by telephone. My mother advised me that she probably had work obligations. That didn't sound like my youngest daughter's character at all. The last time I had stood in my mother's home, Ariel and I still had had such a close bond as mother and daughter. I knew my feelings hadn't changed. I was concerned as well as saddened at the thought of Ariel not making time in her schedule to visit with her sister and me while we were in town. We had traveled such a far distance. I couldn't ignore that familiar, relentless pain in my chest as a result of the anxiety brought on from discouragement and disappointment.

That evening, my mother and stepfather treated my sister, brother-in-law, and Ashley out to dinner. I wished my son, Jacob, my daughter Ariel, my nephew, my stepbrother, and a few other relatives could've joined us. In fact, that evening, I wish I had been more adamant about my stepbrother joining us. Unfortunately, they were all busy with work obligations.

The following day, my mother watched over Ashley for a few hours while I met up with a male acquaintance of mine. Thomas took me for a stroll on the Walk of Fame in Hollywood, California. We stopped to have dinner along the way. I felt more at ease that day. He amused me when he jokingly stated that they were planning to place my name on one of the stars out on the Walk of Fame. As much as I'm sure he was joking, I still thought, *THAT would be absolutely FANTABULOUS! However, I'm not famous for anything...yet.*

The following day, Ashley and I visited Disneyland. We spent the majority of the day there. All was going great until I rolled Ashley aboard the Small World boat ride. We boarded the little tour boat alone. I sat in a seat in front of where Ashley was positioned on the boat in her wheelchair. I turned around to glance at my eldest daughter for a moment. She looked peaceful as the boat set sail, making its way into the tunnel of the building structure, while the theme song played over the sound system. She had ridden this particular ride before on many occasions, since she was a child. However, that's about the moment the thought, *What if this is the last time Ashley ever rides this ride?* crossed my mind. Then as I noticed the empty seats, I thought, *My other two children should be aboard this boat also, just like in the past.* In that moment, instead of reaching for my camera, I became very emotional. It was difficult to choke down my tears. Nonetheless, I prayed that Ashley and the attendants operating on the ride wouldn't notice that I was suddenly an emotional wreck. Had one of the theme park employees noticed, they probably would've wondered what the matter could be. Until that moment, I had never cried at Disneyland before. Quite literally, it took the majority of duration of that ride for me to regain my composure. Once the ride was over, the attendants operating the ride decided to put us through again, just as they had in the past, without being asked. This enabled me to capture a few photographic images as well as video of Ashley aboard the boat.

I attempted to make the rest of the day at the theme park as pleasant as possible, for the two of us.

Over the course of the next two days, we enjoyed "family time" visiting with relatives. Pebble also seemed to enjoy his new surroundings, and he made quite an impression with both my mother, stepfather, and sister.

On one day there, I reserved some time to drive back to the city where my children and I had lived. I drove around the housing development and asked Ashley if the neighborhood looked familiar. I noted that the front yard of our former residence appeared to look a little different. However, we didn't stop to speak with any of our former neighbors.

I drove to the intersection where Ashley's vehicle collision had occurred, noting that the surrounding areas were built up with more structures in comparison to fifteen years ago. There was the same intersection where Ashley had lost her abilities. Yet, she had cheated death, awakened from the coma, and miraculously survived, by the grace of God.

I drove Ashley over to the campus where she had once attended high school, only about two blocks away. We didn't stop to park our vehicle and walk into the school to speak to any of the school faculty. However, I sat there for a few moments reminiscing over a much louder, sassier version of Ashley, as well as how many times I had visited that school campus. I had to laugh at the memory of turning in Ashley's cheerleading audition paperwork while Ashley was only a sophomore. That day, the faculty member collecting the forms thought I was the student auditioning for the cheerleading squad. I politely informed, "No. I'm her parent."

Those few moments were bittersweet.

One evening, we ventured out to the coast and breathed in the crisp, West Coast ocean air, while intently listening to the tide along the shoreline. The sound of the waves was soothing to my spirit. I was heavy-hearted, knowing that our visit to southern California would soon come to an end. We hadn't seen Ariel, and the time was drawing near to return to the East Coast.

Once we set out in route for the state of New York, we left not having seen Ariel. The drive home seemed longer. I wasn't feeling as zealous about the "Girl Power" excursion anymore. Trying to put my emotions aside was difficult.

Nonetheless, Ashley, Pebble, and I made it back across the continent safe and sound.

A Work in Progress

In December 2019, Ashley's biological dad visited us for a few days. They had reconnected by telephone and by means of the internet within the previous year. Yet, Ashley had not seen her dad face-to-face in over a decade.

Before he visited, I told him that he was welcome to visit, as long as he respected my household rules and boundaries. He made travel arrangements while both Ashley and I prepared for a house guest during Christmastime. Her dad advised that he planned to stay with us for a few days during the Christmas season. Therefore, I paid attention to details ahead of time, from grocery and gift shopping, to putting together a small gift set of hygiene supplies and leaving it in the room he'd be staying in during his visit.

I set out a tray of homemade Christmas cookies for him and even made a sign for Ashley to hold on her lap to greet her dad, once he arrived at the airport and made his way down the airport escalator, on the evening of December 24, 2019. I stood off to the side with a video camera ready to roll for their father and daughter reunion.

After leaving the airport and while commuting back home that evening, Ashley's dad rode in the backseat of my vehicle, conversing and then suddenly boasting about being an "atheist." That's the point when I silently speculated in the driver's seat that he wasn't necessarily visiting us because he was interested in seeing his daughter. He wasn't even on New York State soil for an entire hour before he was already trying to instigate a religious dispute with me, on a Christian holiday no less. He had traveled to and arrived in the state of New York without even a change of clothes. At some point I advised him that it might behoove him to book a motel room as well as a rental vehicle in the future during his visits.

Once we arrived at our humble residence, her dad enjoyed the Christmas cookies that I had made. He specifically was impressed and liked the cookies that had windows made out of sugar. We all sat up late that evening, visiting with one another in the living room before retiring to our separate bedrooms. I slept in the guest bed next to Ashley's hospital bed in her room, while giving up my bedroom to her dad for a few days.

On Christmas Day, we opened our gifts together. Later in the afternoon, Ashley celebrated her thirty-fourth birthday with both of her parents. She seemed very happy to have both of her parents present for her special occasion, although she knew very well that he and I did not get along very well. To redirect Kevin's focus, I decided to allow him to review the photograph scrapbook that I had made of Ashley's hospital guest-book. He gladly opened the scrapbook with great anticipation. However, after reading as well as glancing at the photographs and turning through its pages, he was reduced to tears. I was empathetic, understanding in that moment that Kevin was reminded that what had happened to Ashley was *traumatic*. However, she survived, and she has an incredible miracle story. Until that moment, I was not sure how Kevin was coping. However, after being acquainted with him for over thirty-five years, I think that night was the first time I ever seen him cry.

The following day, I offered to drive him to a thrift store as well as a local retail store so he could purchase some clothing for himself. He advised me he was expecting a shipment of clothes from the Midwest that he had had a friend of his send out. However, he still accepted my offer. We ventured out into the village to go shopping. In the interim, I allowed him to borrow and wear a few things that belonged to my son: a football jersey and flannel pajama bottoms.

During his stay, I politely advised him that he wasn't staying at a bed-and-breakfast. Therefore, in the event he got hungry, there was ample food in the residence for him to prepare his own meals. I reminded him that catering to him was not my responsibility, while I tended to my daughter's care, the household chores, etc. Due to the circumstances and our past history, my mother concurred with me.

Kevin left a few short days later, returning to the Midwest, after quickly wearing out his welcome. Before he left, he advised me he thought that would be the last time he'd ever see Ashley. While he was with us, he didn't seem sad...just tense and tired. It appeared that he had trouble relaxing. He commented about many things, including how beautiful of a county Ashley and I currently reside in.

I was fortunate to get both him and Ashley over to visit an aquarium out in the city, to create a positive family memory for her. But during his visit, several disputes occurred. We argued over a multitude of different things, which dated all the way back to the year 1987, over matters that required being resolved. In such a manner, the moment when he insisted on insulting me once again in my residence in front of Ashley, I ended up finally punching him in the face. Throughout the course of time, I've never harbored ill will or resentment toward Kevin. However, I don't appreciate being the subject of his consistent disrespect. I've always tried being civil to him, for the sake of Ashley, because I know she loves both of us, even if Kevin no longer wants to be part of her life. That is a personal choice he has made for himself and one he'll have to live with for the rest of his life. It's not a decision imposed upon him. That being said, it's obvious he has no idea what I've gone through to keep Ashley alive. He's apathetic to the multitude of challenges and struggles that I've had to address, a few that were the result of his own lies from long ago. This is frustrating. Kevin is the sort of stressor that I don't have the time or the patience for. Nonetheless, he should feel fortunate that I transported him back to the airport.

When we drove home from the airport, I couldn't help wondering what Ashley was thinking, but she was not able to verbalize her thoughts and feelings pertaining to the arguments, especially over what her dad had said. However, neither did she look upset that he was gone. During moments such as this, I remind Ashley that there's a heavenly Father who loves her. God is interested in everything going on within her life. I also remind her that I love her. My prayer, as a mother, is that my daughter believes me and doesn't internalize the negative, thoughtless comments from others.

Kevin's shipment of clothing arrived a few days after he left. Without even opening and looking into the box, I returned the parcel back to him in an expedient manner.

Outreach ministry, I've noted, is a subject in which my mother excels, even though she doesn't attend church regularly. My mother has a history of being a very generous individual. I also participate in outreach ministry. However, I've learned there are two types of recipient personalities in the world: those who truly appreciate the help when it is needed. These people move on with their lives, and perhaps eventually they also participate in outreach ministry once things are going better within their own lives.

The other type of recipient doesn't appreciate anything another person has done for them. They take advantage of the diligent good works while always seeking something more that they can take. I've learned to be more selective pertaining to whom I help and whom I don't. With regard to outreach ministry, I know the normal response from most appreciative recipients is a humble, genuine "Thank you." That being said, I strive to treat everyone with dignity and respect unless they are a consistent problem. I expect respect be reciprocated. Otherwise, I simply dissociate to avoid unnecessary conflict.

Am I a perfect Christian and mother? No. Do I regret some of the decisions I've made in Ashley's life? Yes. There are a few things I think I would've done differently, had I known what the outcome would've been ahead of time. Just like everyone else in this world, I'm a work in progress. However, like God, I'm interested in what's going on in each of my children's lives. The important thing is that Ashley's still alive. Therefore, I must be doing quite a few things right, despite what harsh critics have to say.

Hope

As the New Year of 2020 rang in, Ashley and I prepared for countless professional appointments, including attending a few political events both out of state and within our small town. I found myself reaching out, via the internet, to a few politicians over important matters that needed to be resolved, even though I'm no political guru by any stretch of the means.

Shortly thereafter, both Ashley and I attended a political event dinner party. We dressed up that night and enjoyed fraternizing with those who also attended the dinner party. I noted Ashley was the only individual present who was confined to a wheelchair. I was moved by a speech that night, an individual who was giving reverence to God as well as Christianity while stating he wanted to do his part in helping to make America great again. As he spoke, I couldn't help but think of the American Revolution having been fought on the very ground where we had met for such an event.

I think most citizens aren't concerned about their constitutional rights until someone infringes upon them. However, if that occurs, I think most citizens still wouldn't know what to do. That's why I believe it's necessary to elect those who are willing to defend the citizens as well as uphold the constitutional rights of all Americans. I think it's important to thwart anyone or anything that schemes to jeopardize that.

Meanwhile, upon the turn of the New Year, I also consulted with a publishing office pertaining to the book that I was writing and working on over the course of several years. Therefore, I submitted an entry to their offices. Within a few short days, I was ecstatic to learn their offices were very interested to publish my work. In such a way, I let out a cheer and advised Ashley as well as other relatives at once.

I had read, via the internet, that a particular church group was looking for five hundred Christians to appear as an "extra" in a faith-based Christian film that was scheduled for filming later in the year out in the state of California. I submitted an entry on a whim and later found that my entry was accepted, much to my surprise. I waited in anticipation for the scheduled dates of filming so I could synchronize my schedule accordingly and plan for a relative to assist with Ashley's care during the filming process.

However, *then* I received notification from a local church, out on the East Coast, asking if I'd be interested in preaching at their church a few Sundays each month. I advised them I'd be glad to minister at their church. Immediately, I started purchasing supplies and secured a date, while praying about and contemplating an inspirational message to preach to their congregation. It appeared my great plans to be an extra in a Christian film were suddenly postponed. However, I was okay with that, since I knew I was called to minister for the purpose of kingdom building. Nonetheless, I informed the director of the film that I probably wasn't going to be able to make it to the set the first week of filming, after all.

During the month of March, I turned 51 years old. I awakened that morning feeling tired, downtrodden, and not in the mood to celebrate at all. In fact, I would have been okay if I could've stayed in bed the entire day, without having to address any responsibilities and discovered all my woes were suddenly resolved. Nonetheless, God gave me the strength to get out of bed and make myself a pot of coffee to drink, in order to courageously face another day and all the responsibilities associated with it. I don't think people truly understand the tasks that I go through in order to leave the house with Ashley for even just a few minutes, ensuring we *both* look presentable. Nonetheless, we ventured out into the village on the afternoon of my birthday, so I could simply purchase myself a birthday cake and a bouquet of pink roses, named "Hot Princess." After I returned to my residence, I had to laugh upon noticing the name of the roses, while carefully arranging each rose stem in a vase within my kitchen. I thought, *Someone has a very cute sense of humor.* I couldn't help but wonder who had been delegated the responsibility of naming the bouquets of flowers within the grocery store's floral department. Then I pondered, *Am I the only individual who wonders about such things?* Since becoming a full-time personal assistant and caregiver, residing in a small town, having few friends as well as relatives, if there is anything that I have had a lot of time for it is... time to think. I have ample time to get alone with God, being cautious about who I become friends with and who I don't, omitting those from my life who do not want to see me attain my goals, or who do not share the same religious beliefs or thoughts pertaining to family as I do, while practicing my gifts and skills, and discovering my hidden talents.

Later within the month of March, mainstream media announced the global Coronavirus pandemic (aka: COVID-19) crisis. Therefore, Countless panicked individuals rushed to the retail stores, purchasing paper products such as toilet paper and other supplies, leaving store shelves across the nation quite literally bare.

During that time, Ashley helped me select the design of the book cover. We sat there for several moments admiring the artistry of each design presented to us. While we reviewed our option's, I had Christian music playing over the stereo. Once we concurred on a book cover, I couldn't help but notice the song playing over the stereo in that very moment was King of Heaven. I sat quietly next to Ashley, at the dining table, staring at the book cover selection and listening to said song. We notified the publishers office right away to inform them of our selection before I busied myself with drafting plans pertaining to an entirely different project associated with this book. This phase was an exciting time for both Ashley and I, redirecting our attention from what was going on out in the world for a few moments.

Within a few short weeks as citizens learned more about the actual threat of COVID-19, mandatory "Social Distancing" and Quarantine went into effect. Citizens were encouraged to stay home to reduce the risk of becoming infected. Entertainers video recorded themselves and posted their videos via internet as a way to encourage the general public to stay calm. While others offered prayer, bible study, read books aloud and so forth. While countless Church Buildings, State Departments, schools, retail stores, movie theatres, theme parks, beauty salons, restaurants, etc. across The United States had to close for an indefinite period of time. Military Bases were also on mandatory "Lock Down" under Quarantine. Music concerts as well as other events were "cancelled", until further notice. Healthcare employees were working overtime. Volunteer Christian Ministry teams, set up hospital tents, outside of hospitals, to assist with providing care to patients.

All plans that I had in early March of 2020, pertaining to preaching at a church, attending music concerts and then traveling out-of-state to be an extra in a faith-based film, were also abruptly "cancelled" and/ or postponed. One evening, I sat next to Ashley in her hospital bed. I literally cried watching video footage of Disneyland theme park, closed and appearing like an abandoned ghost town, from an aerial view.

State Governors nationwide mandated citizens to wear surgical face masks or some other face covering (such as a bandana) in order to enter in establishments that were allowed to remain open during the pandemic. Some citizens blatantly chose to not comply. While Ashley cried not understanding, at first, why I attempted to keep her in partial, self-appointed, quarantine and why we weren't visiting some of the usual places we frequent. Ashley conveyed she was bored. I explained I was trying to keep her well. Then I busied myself with putting together a care package together for Ariel and sent it out right away. Enclosed were waterproof facemasks, Nitrile exam gloves and a few other items. As the weeks of the Pandemic swept the world, I experienced some difficulty in finding a few medical supply items that I need in order to do my job adequately. I stopped at around 5 stores within the county I reside in before I could find the few items I needed to purchase; Exam Gloves and Isopropyl Rubbing Alcohol.

I prayed my two other children were staying well; Ariel within the city that she resides in as well as Jacob stationed out on a United States military base somewhere. I prayed researchers within the field of Medicine would be capable of finding an antidote in the near future and that those diagnosed with the COVID-19 infirmity would be healed. My prayers were partly answered within a matter of days, as mainstream media announced an antidote was created. However, enough medicine wasn't available for the general public at that time. It was forecasted it would be close to a year before enough medicine/vaccination could be produced and available. Therefore, I prayed researchers would be enabled to produce more medicine in a shorter period of time than they had originally anticipated. By early

June of 2020 over 370,000 New Yorkers were diagnosed with said infirmity. Throughout the world, some of those which were infected by COVID-19, were dying. COVID-19 was thought of and referred to as a "plague". A plague like never before seen in this generation. Also referred to as an "Invisible Enemy". Some folks were irritable and negative. While others panicked. Meanwhile, both Ashley and I did our best to practice "Social Distancing" and stayed calm. We were fortunate to have not run out of necessary supplies. We didn't participate, neither contribute to, the mass chaos going on out at the grocery stores.

Every Day Is a Gift from God

Ashley posing with daisies in Lily Park, 2020

Had I known that warm October morning back in 2004 that it would be the last time I'd see a vibrant Ashley walking around and hearing her beautiful voice, I would've never answered the telephone. I was the last one to see Ashley in her whole condition. I was the last one to speak with Ashley before her vehicle collision. *That* is the reality that I have to live with every single day. I've spent the last fifteen years, protecting that child, reminding her that she is loved unconditionally and making her feel wanted and accepted. Since that day, I've watched the number of her friends and family members slowly diminish and leave the fold. I've contended with challenges I never anticipated. However, despite unwelcome opposition and apathy, somehow I've managed to keep the faith.

When I look at Ashley and observe the expression of her eyes, in comparison to the way it was before her vehicle collision, I see someone who has endured as well as survived *real* physical and emotional pain. Yet, the countenance of her face reveals an individual of grace and natural beauty. She is calm, content, and meek, despite overwhelming conflicts/opposition. She's 100 percent reliant on someone else to tend to her basic needs each day. Most individuals would be panic-stricken if they awakened and found themselves in a similar situation. Yet, every time I admire her countenance, I see the peace that surpasses all understanding. God is holding her innermost being in a perfect calmness.

Since Ashley emerged from the coma, she has emotionally learned to cope with and accepts her prognosis: quadriplegia, traumatic brain injury, as well as aphonia (otherwise non-verbal; mute). She understands and accepts the fact that her prognosis might never change. However, she knows that if God has further progress in store for her life, she'd welcome that also. Therefore, we remain optimistic. Medical technology is advancing all the time. There might be hope for her restored abilities within the future.

I'm thankful that my daughter awakened having an awareness outside of herself, a genuine interest in others, and an awareness of her surroundings. She isn't numb to pain. She can *feel* real emotions, such as: Joy, love, compassion, disappointment, despair, and anger as most individuals. Therefore, I'm mindful to try to keep her environment as pleasant and stress-free as possible.

As her mother as well as a minister, I'm grateful she loves God and still gives reverence to Him. She's a precious miracle with an incredible testimony, fully aware that she is loved in two realms: unconditionally by a mother, as well as by a heavenly Father who refused to give up on her. I'm thankful that Tuesday, October 12, 2004, wasn't the date of the conclusion of her story. I'm thankful she survived.

Every day is a gift from God.

"The grace of the Lord Jesus Christ, and the love of God, and the communion of the Holy Ghost, be with you all. Amen."
—2 Corinthians 13:14

Ashley posing with bouquet of irises, Schoharie County, NY, 2020

About the Author

W. L. Adams

W. L. Adams has studied Christian ministry for over thirty-two years and is tentatively an ordained minister, author, artist, and mother residing within central

New York. She is a full-time personal assistant, with twenty-eight years' experience in the field of health care, having obtained most of her formal education and training in the Midwest as well as on the West Coast. Ms. Adams is a former Auxiliary Associate of the Scho- harie Fire Dept.

On occasion, she volunteers at a museum located in upstate New York, reciting brief history lectures, and she is avid about encouraging citizens to courageously defend their constitutional rights within the United States of America.